ALASKA TRAVEL GUIDE 2025

Your Updated Trip Planner to Exploring Anchorage, Fairbanks, Juneau, and Beyond, with Top Destinations and Practical Tips for an Unforgettable Adventure in the Last Frontier

Albert N. Allred

Disclaimer

Welcome to your **Alaska Travel Guide 2025**! Get ready to explore the Last Frontier with this comprehensive guide, filled with insider tips and must-see destinations. From the soaring peaks of Denali to the icy waters of Glacier Bay, we'll help you uncover the magic of Alaska.

Keep in mind that Alaska's wild spirit can lead to changes in prices, hours, and tour schedules. For a seamless adventure, double-check key details with your chosen hotels, tour operators, and attractions before you go.

Think of this guide as your Alaskan companion, leading you to unforgettable experiences. With a little planning, your trip to the Last Frontier will be everything you've ever imagined.

Happy travels!

Table of Contents

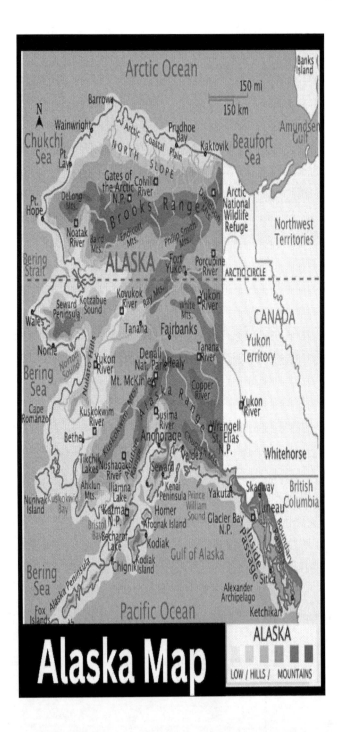

Introduction

Hey fellow adventurers!

So you're thinking about Alaska, huh? Awesome! I've been lucky enough to visit this amazing place many times, and let me tell you, it's like nowhere else on Earth. Every single trip, I discover something new and fall even more in love with the wild beauty of the Last Frontier.

My trip in 2024 was extra special. It was like Alaska opened its arms and welcomed me in, sharing its secrets and showing me just how incredible it truly is.

One of my favorite memories? Stumbling upon a hidden lake in Wrangell-St. Elias National Park. Picture this: sparkling turquoise water surrounded by giant mountains and glaciers. It felt like I'd found a secret paradise! (And guess what? You can find it too!)

Another unforgettable experience was kayaking in Prince William Sound. I woke up before the sun, hopped in my kayak, and paddled through a misty fjord. Everything was so peaceful and quiet. I could hear the water gently lapping against my kayak, and every now and then, a salmon would jump out of the water. At one point, I even saw a bald eagle swoop down and grab a fish! It was like something out of a movie.

Of course, no trip to Alaska is complete without seeing the Northern Lights. I was lucky enough to catch them in Fairbanks this year. Imagine this: you're snuggled up in a cozy cabin, looking up at the sky through a huge window. Suddenly, the whole sky lights up with these amazing colors – green, purple, pink – swirling and dancing around. It's like a magical light show in the sky!

But Alaska is more than just beautiful scenery. It's the people I met along the way that made my trip truly special. I spent an afternoon with a dog musher (someone who races sled dogs) and learned all about how they train their dogs. I hung out with some fishermen in Ketchikan and we swapped stories while eating delicious fresh salmon. And in a small village near Juneau, I learned how to smoke salmon from a local who's been doing it her whole life.

These are the kinds of moments that make Alaska so special. It's not just about seeing amazing things, it's about the experiences you have and the people you meet.

So, what are you waiting for? Grab this guide, start planning your trip, and get ready for an adventure you'll never forget! Who knows, maybe we'll bump into each other on the trail someday!

Chapter 1: Discovering The Last Frontier

A. A Brief History of Alaska

Alaska's story began long, long ago when the first people crossed over from Asia, walking the Bering Land Bridge into this untamed land around 14,000 years ago. These early Alaskans, ancestors of the Inuit, Tlingit, and other indigenous groups, learned to thrive here, creating cultures that embraced the land's rugged beauty. They developed lifestyles around fishing, hunting, and close-knit communities, passing down stories and traditions that are still celebrated today.

Fast forward to the 18th century, when Russian explorers landed on Alaska's shores, captivated by the wealth of fur-bearing animals like the prized sea otters. The Russians saw Alaska as a goldmine—not for gold itself, but for fur. They set up trading posts and brought the Russian Orthodox Church with them, building the first settlements on islands like Kodiak. But their arrival wasn't without hardship; native communities faced challenges, with new diseases and conflicts affecting their lives. Yet, they held on, adapting as they always had.

In 1867, Alaska's story took a surprising turn when Russia sold it to the United States for $7.2 million. Can you imagine the mixed reactions? People called it "Seward's Folly" after Secretary of State William Seward, thinking Alaska was just a frozen wasteland. But little did they know, Seward's purchase would become one of America's biggest treasures. Within a few decades, gold was discovered, setting off the Klondike Gold Rush and drawing thousands of hopeful miners. Towns popped up almost overnight, filled with prospectors and dreamers ready to make their fortunes. Alaska was no longer a forgotten frontier; it was the land of opportunity.

During World War II, Alaska's strategic importance became clear when Japanese forces occupied two Aleutian Islands. Suddenly, this remote state was on the frontlines, sparking a wave of military activity. Radar stations and airbases were built, and Alaska's proximity to the Soviet Union made it a vital part of U.S. defence during the Cold War. Alaska was no longer just about resources—it was now a key player in national security.

In 1959, Alaska officially became the 49th state, and the discovery of oil in Prudhoe Bay brought a new boom. The Trans-Alaska Pipeline was built to transport oil across the state, transforming Alaska's economy. But with this prosperity came challenges, too. Debates over conservation and land rights arose, and Alaska's indigenous communities stepped forward to ensure their voices were heard, leading to the historic Alaska Native Claims Settlement Act in 1971.

Today, Alaska's rich history is woven into every part of its identity. From Russian churches to gold rush towns and Native Alaskan cultural festivals, the state is a living mosaic of resilience and diversity.

B. Why Visit Alaska in 2025

If you're thinking about visiting Alaska in 2025, get ready for an unforgettable adventure! Alaska is one of those rare places that's just as amazing in person as you imagine, and 2025 is shaping up to be an especially great year to go. Let's talk about why this is the year to plan that bucket-list trip.

Easier Access and New Developments

Alaska's been making travel easier and better than ever. In 2025, you'll find new cruise ship docks, more flight options, and a boost in travel infrastructure. That means getting here is more convenient, whether you're coming for a quick visit or a big, week-long adventure. These updates make exploring the wilderness, charming towns, and national parks that much smoother.

Incredible Natural Wonders

Let's be real—Alaska's natural beauty is something you have to see to believe. And in 2025, you're in for a treat if you've always wanted to catch the Northern Lights. Thanks to high solar activity, the auroras are expected to be extra bright and colourful this year. Imagine looking up and seeing waves of green, purple, and pink lights dance across the sky. It's something you'll remember forever.

Unique Wildlife Experiences

Few places let you get as close to nature as Alaska does. Whether you're watching bears fishing for salmon, spotting whales along the coast, or seeing bald eagles soaring overhead, Alaska's wildlife is simply amazing. In 2025, conservation efforts have kept these animal populations thriving, so your chances of seeing them are better than ever.

Cultural Festivals and Local Traditions

Alaska isn't just about the outdoors; it's also rich in culture. Throughout the year, you'll find festivals that celebrate Alaska's indigenous heritage, art, and traditions. If you're there in March, you can watch the famous Iditarod, a thrilling dog sled race that celebrates Alaska's history and adventurous spirit. These events are a fun way to connect with local traditions and meet people from all walks of life.

Eco-Friendly and Sustainable Travel

If you're a nature lover who cares about the environment, Alaska is perfect. In 2025, more eco-friendly tours and accommodations make it easy to explore responsibly. You can support local communities, respect the wilderness, and still enjoy all Alaska has to offer.

C. Climate and Best Times to Visit

When it comes to Alaska, each season has something totally unique to offer. Depending on what kind of experience you're after, timing your trip just right can make all the difference. Let's break it down so you can pick the season that feels perfect for you.

June to August

If you're all about endless days and outdoor activities, then summer is the time to visit Alaska. Picture this: daylight stretching up to 20 hours, mild temperatures, and perfect conditions for hiking, fishing, and exploring national parks. Temps are generally comfortable, ranging from the 60s to 80s °F, and you'll have more time to soak it all in thanks to those long, golden hours of sunlight. This is Alaska's high season, so things are lively, and it's the best time to catch all the outdoor festivals and wildlife sightings. Just a heads-up, though—it's a popular time to visit, so book early to get the best spots!

September to October

Now, if you love a bit of peace and Alaska's landscapes painted in autumn hues, fall might be your sweet spot. September brings beautiful shades of gold and orange, and the temperatures start to cool down, usually sitting between 40-60°F. It's quieter, which means you get more space to roam and take in the views. And if you've always wanted to see the Northern Lights, fall offers your first chances! Head up north, maybe around Fairbanks, and you might just catch those magical lights filling up the sky.

November to March

Dreaming of a snowy escape? Winter in Alaska is like stepping into a postcard, with snow-covered landscapes and crisp, clear nights perfect for viewing the Northern Lights. Yes, it's cold (think -20°F to 20°F in some places), so pack warmly! This season is all about unique experiences: dog sledding, ice fishing, skiing, and more. And because it's less crowded, you'll have more of Alaska's wild beauty to yourself. Just imagine a quiet night under the auroras—something you won't soon forget.

April to May

Spring in Alaska is a bit of a hidden gem. As the snow melts and temperatures begin to rise (usually into the 30s-50s °F), Alaska comes back to life. Wildlife starts to emerge, the landscapes turn green, and you'll get a sense of the state waking up from winter. It's a fantastic time for birdwatching and spotting newborn animals. Plus, it's not as busy, so you'll enjoy a relaxed, peaceful vibe and more affordable options for travel and stays.

So, When's Your Perfect Time?

Each season in Alaska is special in its own way. If it's your first visit and you want the classic experience, go for summer. For a quieter vibe and stunning colours, fall is a great choice. Winter is a magical time if you want snow and the Northern Lights, while spring gives you that fresh, peaceful Alaska charm. No matter when you choose, Alaska's beauty and wild spirit will be waiting to greet you!

D. Essential Packing Tips for All Seasons

Let's go over some essentials to pack, no matter when you're visiting.

Layers, Layers, Layers

Alaska's weather can change on a dime, even in summer. The best way to be ready for anything? Layers! Start with a good base layer that keeps you warm but wicks away moisture—think a nice thermal top in winter or a lightweight option in summer. Next, add an insulating layer like a fleece or down jacket. Top it all off with a waterproof and windproof outer layer, especially if you're planning on hiking or spending time near the coast. This way, you can adjust your outfit throughout the day as temperatures change.

Footwear: Sturdy and Waterproof

Whether you're visiting in summer or winter, good shoes are a must. A pair of waterproof hiking boots will keep your feet warm and dry, whether you're trekking through snowy trails, muddy paths, or rocky terrain. If you're coming in winter, consider insulated boots to handle the colder temperatures. And don't forget comfortable socks—wool is always a great choice to keep feet warm and dry!

Rain Gear (Yes, Even in Summer)

Alaska is known for its unpredictable rain, so a lightweight rain jacket and rain pants are key, even in the warmer months. These will keep you dry without making you feel too warm if a sudden shower hits. A small, packable umbrella can be a good backup too, though it might be tricky to use on windy days.

Accessories: Sun Protection and Cold-Weather Gear

Sun protection might not be the first thing that comes to mind when you think of Alaska, but in summer, those long daylight hours can be intense. Pack a good hat, sunglasses, and sunscreen to keep yourself safe. For winter, make sure to bring warm accessories—think hats, gloves, scarves, and maybe even hand warmers if you're heading into especially cold areas. It's better to have them and not need them than to be caught shivering!

Insect Repellent for Summer Trips

Yes, Alaska has mosquitoes, and in the summer, they can be pretty relentless, especially in areas near water. A good insect repellent will be your best friend if you're planning on camping, hiking, or spending time near rivers and lakes.

Binoculars and a Camera

You'll probably find yourself surrounded by amazing wildlife and jaw-dropping scenery, so having binoculars and a decent camera can make your trip even more memorable. Whether you're spotting whales, bears, or the Northern Lights, these tools will help you capture the best of Alaska's beauty.

A Reusable Water Bottle

Exploring Alaska can be thirsty work, so make sure you have a reusable water bottle with you. Most towns and parks have places where you can refill, and it's a good way to stay hydrated and reduce plastic waste.

With these essentials in your bag, you'll be ready for whatever Alaska throws your way.

Chapter 2: Getting to Alaska

A. Flights and Transportation Options

Getting to Alaska by air is one of the easiest and most convenient ways to start your adventure. Alaska may feel like the edge of the world, but with multiple airports and plenty of direct flights, it's closer than you might think. Here's what you need to know about flying to Alaska.

Airports and Key Hubs

Anchorage's Ted Stevens Anchorage International Airport

Ted Stevens Anchorage Intern...

5000 W International Airport Rd,
Anchorage, AK 99502, United States

4.5 ★★★★★

View larger map

Ted Stevens Anchorage International Airport

The Local Google

Keyboard shortcuts　Map data ©2024 Google　Terms

Ted Stevens Anchorage Intern...

SCAN THE QR CODE

1. Open your device camera app.
2. Position the QR code in the camera frame.
3. Hold your phone steady.
4. Wait for the code to be recognized.
5. Once recognized, tap on the notification or follow the prompt to access the content or action associated with the Qr code

Anchorage's Ted Stevens Anchorage International Airport (ANC) is the main gateway to Alaska for most travellers, with regular flights from major U.S. cities like Seattle, Chicago, Denver, and Los Angeles. Located just a few miles from downtown Anchorage, it's a modern airport that makes the transition from plane to Alaskan adventure as smooth as possible. If you're heading further north, Fairbanks International Airport (FAI) is another key hub, especially if you want to experience the Arctic, see the Northern Lights, or explore the interior.

Airlines and Routes

You'll find several major airlines flying direct to Alaska. Alaska Airlines is the most popular carrier, with frequent flights to Anchorage and Fairbanks, but other airlines like Delta, United, and American Airlines also have direct routes. From Seattle, you can even find flights that take you straight to smaller cities like Juneau or Ketchikan. During the summer, there are additional seasonal flights to cater to the tourist season, making it easy to plan your trip.

Booking and Costs

Ticket prices can vary depending on the season, but you can generally find round-trip flights to Anchorage from the lower 48 states starting around $300 to $600 if you book early. Summer is Alaska's high season, so prices are likely to be a bit higher from June through August. If you're visiting in the off-season, particularly in winter, flights can be significantly cheaper. Price comparison websites like Google Flights, Skyscanner, and directly through airline websites can help you find the best deals.

Airport Facilities and Services

Anchorage and Fairbanks airports are well-equipped for travellers, with plenty of amenities to make your arrival comfortable. You'll find car rental services, duty-free shops, restaurants, and even art displays showcasing Alaskan culture. If you're arriving at Anchorage and need transportation, there are taxis and shuttle services readily available, with fares to downtown Anchorage generally around $20-$30.

Useful Contacts and Websites

- Ted Stevens Anchorage International Airport: (www.anchorageairport.com)
- Alaska Airlines: (www.alaskaair.com)
- Fairbanks International Airport: (www.fairbanksairport.com)

B. Arriving by Cruise Ship

If you love the idea of starting your Alaskan adventure on the water, then arriving by cruise ship might just be perfect for you. Cruising to Alaska is like a vacation within a vacation – you get the thrill of exploring a new place every day, but with all the comforts of your ship.

Which Cruise Lines Go to Alaska?

There are lots of great options to choose from, like Princess Cruises, Holland America, Royal Caribbean, and Norwegian Cruise Line. Most Alaska cruises leave from Seattle or Vancouver, taking you through the Inside Passage. This route is famous for its peaceful channels, beautiful islands, and chances to spot wildlife along the way. Depending on the itinerary, your cruise might stop at amazing towns like Juneau, Ketchikan, Sitka, or Skagway, where you can explore Alaska's unique culture and landscapes.

Choosing the Right Cruise for You

Not all Alaska cruises are the same, so it's worth picking one that matches what you want. Most itineraries are around 7 days, which gives you a nice taste of Alaska. But if you have more time, there are longer cruises that include extra stops and scenic spots like Glacier Bay or Hubbard Glacier. Some cruises focus more on the scenic parts, perfect if you're all about the views, while others pack in fun shore excursions like whale watching, dog sledding, or glacier hikes. Whatever your style, there's a cruise that fits.

What to Expect at Each Port

Every port in Alaska has its own special vibe. In Juneau, you can hop off the ship and find yourself right in the heart of downtown, with cute shops, local restaurants, and easy access to the famous Mendenhall Glacier. Ketchikan is known for its totem poles and fishing history – you can even join a fishing excursion if you're up for it. Skagway feels like stepping back in time, with wooden boardwalks and old-fashioned buildings from the gold rush days. Each stop has something different, so be ready to explore!

Shore Excursions to Make Your Trip Even Better

One of the best things about cruising to Alaska is the shore excursions. Picture yourself flying over glaciers in a helicopter, watching bears in the wild, or kayaking along a quiet bay. Excursions like these let you get up close with Alaska's wild side. You can book through the cruise line, but sometimes booking with local companies can give you a more personal experience. Either way, it's worth planning a few must-do activities to really make the most of each stop.

How Much Does It Cost?

Prices can vary, but a 7-day cruise usually starts around $800 per person for a basic room. If you want a balcony with those amazing views, expect to pay more. And keep an eye out for deals – booking early or during the off-season can save you a bit. Websites like Cruise.com or the cruise line's site can help you compare prices and find the best fit.

Useful Links to Help You Plan

- Princess Cruises: (www.princess.com)
- Holland   America: (www.hollandamerica.com)
- Royal   Caribbean: (www.royalcaribbean.com)
- Norwegian Cruise Line: (www.ncl.com)

Chapter 3: Top Destinations in Alaska

A. Anchorage

Alaska's largest city, is a vibrant blend of urban life and natural beauty, offering visitors a unique experience where modern amenities meet the rugged wilderness.

Location and History

Situated in south-central Alaska, Anchorage lies along the Cook Inlet, surrounded by the Chugach Mountains. Established in 1914 as a railroad construction port, it rapidly developed into a key transportation and economic hub. Today, Anchorage serves as a gateway to Alaska's vast landscapes and diverse cultures.

Getting There

Most travelers arrive via Ted Stevens Anchorage International Airport (ANC), located about 5 miles from downtown. The airport accommodates numerous domestic and international flights, making it a convenient entry point. For those exploring Alaska by road, Anchorage is accessible via the Glenn and Seward Highways, connecting it to other major destinations.

Things to Do

- Explore the Anchorage Museum: Delve into Alaska's art, history, and science through engaging exhibits. Open daily from 10 AM to 6 PM. Admission is $20 for adults, $15 for seniors and students, and $10 for children aged 6-12. Tickets can be purchased online at [www.anchoragemuseum.org].

- Visit the Alaska Native Heritage Center: Experience indigenous cultures through performances, crafts, and storytelling. Open May through September, 9 AM to 5 PM. Admission is $24.95 for adults and $16.95 for children aged 7-16. More information is available at [www.alaskanative.net].

- Hike Flattop Mountain: A popular trail offering panoramic views of the city and surrounding landscapes. The trailhead is about a 20-minute drive from downtown. Parking is $5 per vehicle.

- Stroll the Tony Knowles Coastal Trail: An 11-mile scenic path ideal for walking, biking, or wildlife spotting. Bike rentals are available downtown, with rates around $20 per hour.

Where to Stay

- Hotel Captain Cook: A luxury hotel located downtown, offering rooms starting at $250 per night. Amenities include multiple restaurants, a fitness center, and stunning views. Reservations can be made at [www.captaincook.com].

- Alyeska Resort: Located about 40 miles from Anchorage in Girdwood, this resort offers a mountain retreat with rooms starting at $300 per night. Features include a spa, fine dining, and access to outdoor activities. Book at [www.alyeskaresort.com].

Dining Options

- Moose's Tooth Pub and Pizzeria: Famous for its craft beers and gourmet pizzas. A meal for two averages $40. Located at 3300 Old Seward Hwy. More details at [www.moosestooth.net](https.

- Snow City Café: A popular spot for breakfast and brunch, known for its hearty portions and local ingredients. Expect to spend around $15 per person. Located at 1034 W 4th Ave. Visit [www.snowcitycafe.com] for more information.

Best Time to Visit

Summer (June to August) offers mild temperatures ranging from 55°F to 70°F, extended daylight hours, and numerous festivals. Winter (December to February) provides opportunities for snow sports and viewing the Northern Lights, with temperatures between 5°F and 30°F.

Additional Information

- Visitor Information Center: Located at 546 W 4th Ave, open daily from 9 AM to 5 PM. Contact them at (907) 257-2363 or visit [www.anchorage.net].

- Public Transportation: People Mover buses operate throughout the city, with fares at $2 per ride. Schedules and routes are available at [www.muni.org/Departments/transit]

B. Fairbanks

Welcome to Fairbanks, Alaska's Golden Heart City! Known for its rich gold mining history and as the gateway to the Arctic, Fairbanks offers visitors a mix of outdoor adventures, local culture, and one of the best chances to see the Northern Lights. If you're looking for an authentic Alaskan experience that combines nature, history, and culture, Fairbanks might just steal your heart.

Location and a Bit of History

Fairbanks is located in the interior of Alaska, about 360 miles north of Anchorage. Founded in 1901, this city got its start during Alaska's gold rush and quickly became a key trading post. Named after Charles W. Fairbanks, a U.S. senator who later became vice president, Fairbanks grew as miners poured into the area seeking their fortunes. Today, it's a city that celebrates its frontier past while embracing the vibrant, modern community it's become.

How to Get There

You can reach Fairbanks by air, road, or train. Most visitors fly into Fairbanks International Airport (FAI), which has direct flights from several major U.S. cities, especially during the peak travel seasons. If you're coming from Anchorage, you can also take the scenic drive along the Parks Highway or board the Alaska Railroad for a stunning, all-day train ride through breathtaking landscapes.

What to Do in Fairbanks

- Chase the Northern Lights: Fairbanks is one of the best places in the world to see the aurora borealis. The best time for viewing is between September and April, when dark, clear skies give you the highest chance of catching the magical lights. For an unforgettable experience, consider staying at an aurora lodge or joining a guided aurora tour.

- Visit the Museum of the North: Located on the University of Alaska Fairbanks campus, this museum is a must-see. It houses everything from indigenous art and Alaskan wildlife exhibits to fascinating displays on Arctic exploration. Open year-round, admission is around $16 for adults, with discounts for seniors, students, and children.

- Step Back in Time at Pioneer Park: This historic park celebrates Fairbanks' gold rush days with old-time cabins, a steam-powered riverboat, and interactive displays. Entry to the park is free, though some attractions within may charge a small fee. It's open from mid-May to early September, making it perfect for summer visitors.

Where to Stay

Fairbanks has options for all types of travellers, from budget stays to cozy lodges:

- Chena Hot Springs Resort: About an hour from Fairbanks, this resort offers a relaxing escape with its natural hot springs, famous year-round for a warm soak under the Alaskan sky. Rates start around $200 per night, and they offer aurora viewing tours in the winter. Book through their site at [www.chenahotsprings.com].

- Bridgewater Hotel: Located downtown, this hotel provides a central base with easy access to Fairbanks' main attractions. Rooms start at $150, making it a comfortable and convenient option. You can book through [www.fountainheadhotels.com/bridgewat er].

- Pike's Waterfront Lodge: Set along the Chena River, this lodge offers charming rooms and cabin-style accommodations starting around $180 per night. Pike's has an eco-friendly focus and even has its own aurora conservatory for winter guests. Visit [www.pikeslodge.com] to book.

Where to Eat and Drink

Fairbanks' food scene may surprise you! Here are a few favourites:

- The Pump House Restaurant: With a cosy atmosphere and a riverside location, this spot is famous for its fresh Alaskan seafood and hearty game dishes. Dinner for two costs around $70. Reservations recommended at [www.pumphousealaska.com].

- Lavelle's Bistro: A favourite for locals and visitors alike, Lavelle's serves up gourmet dishes with a twist, perfect for a special night out. Expect to pay around $60 for two. Check them out at [www.lavellesbistro.com].

- Big Daddy's BBQ & Banquet Hall: If you're in the mood for something casual, Big Daddy's is a popular BBQ spot with generous portions and friendly service. Meals here start around $15 per person. More details at [www.bigdaddysbbqalaska.com].

Best Time to Visit

For winter travellers, mid-September to April offers prime aurora viewing and winter sports, though temperatures can dip below -20°F, so bundle up! Summer, from June to August, brings long daylight hours, mild temperatures, and the Midnight Sun Festival, which fills Fairbanks with music, food, and festivities. Hotel prices and tours are a bit pricier in summer, so booking early is a good idea.

Helpful Contacts

- Fairbanks Visitor Information Center: Located at 101 Dunkel St., open daily from 8 AM to 5 PM. Call (907) 456-5774 or visit [www.explorefairbanks.com].
- Alaska Railroad: For scenic train journeys to Fairbanks, check routes and prices at [www.alaskarailroad.com].
- Aurora Forecast and Tours: For up-to-date aurora forecasts, check out the Geophysical Institute at [www.gi.alaska.edu/auroraforecast].

C. Juneau

Welcome to Juneau, Alaska's capital city and one of the most unique state capitals in the U.S.! Imagine a place where towering mountains meet icy blue waters, where glaciers are practically in your backyard, and where history and culture are as rich as the surrounding landscape. Accessible only by sea or air, Juneau is the perfect mix of adventure, beauty, and Alaskan charm.

Where It's Located and a Bit of History

Juneau is nestled between the Gastineau Channel and majestic mountains, surrounded by the lush Tongass National Forest. Established during the gold rush in the 1880s, Juneau quickly became a hub for prospectors and miners, transforming over the years into a vibrant town rich with indigenous heritage and local traditions. This capital city is home to around 32,000 people and is known for its stunning scenery, fresh seafood, and the incredible Mendenhall Glacier.

Getting There

Since Juneau is not connected by road to the rest of Alaska, most visitors arrive by air or cruise ship. Juneau International Airport (JNU) has regular flights from Seattle and other major Alaskan cities, making it an easy hop from the mainland. If you're arriving by cruise, Juneau is a popular stop on many Inside Passage itineraries, and you'll be greeted by scenic views of mountains and waters as you approach the port.

What to Do in Juneau

- Visit the Mendenhall Glacier: Just a short drive from downtown, the Mendenhall Glacier is one of Juneau's most iconic sights. Take a walk on the easy, scenic paths around Mendenhall Lake, or, if you're up for more adventure, try one of the guided tours that let you hike on the glacier itself. The Mendenhall Glacier Visitor Center is open year-round, and admission is around $5 per person.

- Explore the Alaska State Museum: This museum is a must for anyone wanting to dive into Alaska's history and native heritage. You'll find exhibits on everything from indigenous art and artifacts to displays on Alaska's Russian and gold rush eras. The museum is open Monday to Saturday, and admission is around $12 for adults.

- Ride the Mount Roberts Tramway: For breathtaking views of Juneau and the surrounding wilderness, take a ride up the Mount Roberts Tramway. Once at the top, you can explore hiking trails, visit the nature center, or enjoy a meal at the Timberline Bar & Grill with panoramic views of the city and channel. Tickets are about $35 per adult and $18 for children, and the tram operates from May to September.

Where to Stay

Juneau offers a variety of accommodations for all budgets:

- Baranof Downtown Hotel: Located right in the heart of downtown Juneau, this historic hotel offers comfortable rooms starting around $180 per night. Book at [www.baranofhotel.com].

- Silverbow Inn & Suites: A boutique inn with charming rooms, complimentary breakfast, and even a rooftop hot tub, Silverbow provides a cozy stay with rooms starting at $160. Visit [www.silverbowinn.com] for reservations.

- <u>Pearson's Pond Luxury Inn and Adventure Spa:</u> For a more unique experience, try this lovely inn surrounded by gardens and ponds. Rates start around $250 per night, and you can book at [www.pearsonspond.com].

Where to Eat and Drink

Juneau is famous for its seafood, and you won't want to miss a meal here!

- <u>Tracy's King Crab Shack:</u> If you're craving fresh king crab, this spot is a must-visit. Known for its crab legs, crab bisque, and friendly service, a meal for two here is around $50. Visit [www.kingcrabshack.com] for hours and menu.

- <u>The Rookery Café:</u> This local favourite offers a great mix of locally-sourced dishes and fresh-baked pastries. You can expect to pay around $30 for a casual lunch or dinner. Check out [www.therookerycafe.com]for more info.

- <u>Red Dog Saloon:</u> A legendary Alaskan watering hole, the Red Dog Saloon has been around since the gold rush era.

Known for its fun atmosphere and hearty pub food, it's a great spot for a casual meal or a drink. Meals start at $20, and you can find more at [www.reddogsaloon.com].

Best Time to Visit

The best time to visit Juneau depends on what you're looking for. Summer, from June to August, brings mild temperatures (averaging 60-70°F) and long daylight hours, perfect for hiking, glacier tours, and outdoor festivals. This is also when cruise season is in full swing, so the town has a lively buzz. If you're more interested in a quieter experience and possibly seeing the Northern Lights, consider visiting in early fall (September) or late spring (May).

Useful Contacts

- Juneau Visitor Center: Located at 800 Glacier Ave, open daily. Call (907) 586-2201 or visit [www.traveljuneau.com] for details.
- Juneau International Airport (JNU): Visit www.juneau.org for flight schedules and airport information.
- Mendenhall Glacier Visitor Center: For details on glacier tours and hours, visit [www.fs.usda.gov/mendenhall].

D. Skagway

Welcome to Skagway, the charming little town that feels like a step back in time to the days of the Klondike Gold Rush. Nestled in a valley with stunning mountains and scenic fjords, Skagway is like Alaska's living museum, where you can walk along boardwalks, visit historic saloons, and imagine the wild days when fortune-seekers rushed here in search of gold. With fewer than 1,000 year-round residents, this town might be small, but it's packed with history, adventure, and charm.

Where It's Located and a Bit of History

Skagway is located in southeast Alaska, near the northern tip of the Inside Passage. Established during the Klondike Gold Rush in 1897, Skagway quickly became a boomtown, serving as a gateway for prospectors heading north to the goldfields. Thousands of fortune-seekers passed through Skagway on their way to the Yukon, making it one of the most important gold rush towns in Alaska. Today, it's a popular stop on cruise routes and a fantastic destination for history lovers and outdoor adventurers alike.

Getting There

Most visitors arrive in Skagway by cruise ship, as it's a staple on Alaska's Inside Passage itineraries. You can also reach Skagway by ferry from Juneau via the Alaska Marine Highway, or if you're up for a scenic road trip, you can drive from Whitehorse, Yukon, in Canada along the Klondike Highway. For those preferring to fly, Skagway has a small airport with flights from Juneau, though availability is limited.

What to Do in Skagway

- Ride the White Pass & Yukon Route Railroad: One of the highlights of any visit to Skagway is the scenic train ride along the historic White Pass & Yukon Route. Originally built in 1898 during the gold rush, this narrow-gauge railway climbs steep mountain passes, crosses trestle bridges, and offers breathtaking views of waterfalls, glaciers, and the lush Alaskan landscape. Tickets range from $95 to $135 for a round trip, and you can book at [www.wpyr.com].

- Explore the Klondike Gold Rush National Historical Park: This park preserves much of Skagway's gold rush history, including restored buildings, museums, and historical exhibits. Start your visit at the visitor center on Broadway Street, where you can learn about the gold rush and pick up a map for a self-guided walking tour of Skagway's historic district. Entrance to the park is free, and it's open daily during the summer season.

- Hike the Chilkoot Trail: If you're up for a real adventure, the Chilkoot Trail is a legendary 33-mile trail that gold-seekers once used on their journey to the Yukon. The trail starts just outside Skagway, and while you don't have to hike the entire distance, even a short hike gives you a sense of the challenges that early miners faced. Guided day hikes are available, and permits are required for overnight treks.

Where to Stay

Skagway has several charming accommodation options, ranging from historic hotels to cozy B&Bs:

- Historic Skagway Inn: This boutique inn has been around since the gold rush days and offers charming rooms with a vintage feel. Rates start around $150 per night, and breakfast is included. Reserve your stay at [www.skagwayinn.com].

- Westmark Inn Skagway: A comfortable hotel located in the heart of town, the Westmark Inn offers easy access to Skagway's main attractions. Rates start around $140 per night. Book at [www.westmarkhotels.com].

- Chilkoot Trail Outpost: For something different, this family-owned lodge is located near the start of the Chilkoot Trail. It's a bit outside of town but offers a rustic and cozy experience. Rates start around $180 per night. More details are available at [www.chilkoottrailoutpost.com].

Where to Eat and Drink

Despite being a small town, Skagway has some great dining spots:

- Skagway Brewing Company: This local favorite serves up hearty burgers, fresh seafood, and their own craft beer. Be sure to try the spruce tip ale, made with hand-picked spruce tips! A meal for two averages around $50. Visit [www.skagwaybrewing.com].

- Red Onion Saloon: Once a brothel during the gold rush, this historic saloon is now a lively spot for a meal and a glimpse into

Skagway's past. Enjoy pizza, sandwiches, and drinks in a setting filled with character. Meals here cost around $20-$30 per person. Find out more at [www.redonionsaloon.com].

- Sweet Tooth Café: A cozy diner perfect for breakfast or a casual lunch. Try the Alaskan salmon chowder or their homemade pies. Meals cost around $15 per person. No website, but you'll find it easily on Broadway Street.

Best Time to Visit

The best time to visit Skagway is from late May to early September, when the weather is mild (50-70°F) and all the attractions, shops, and tours are in full swing. This is also when most cruises stop by, so you'll find the town lively and bustling. If you prefer a quieter experience, early May or late September are good options, though some tours and businesses may have shorter hours.

Useful Contacts

- Skagway Visitor Center: Located at 245 Broadway, open daily during the summer season. Call (907) 983-2854 or visit [www.skagway.com] for information.

- <u>White Pass & Yukon Route Railroad:</u> For train schedules and bookings, visit [www.wpyr.com] or call (800) 343-7373.

Klondike Gold Rush National Historical Park: Check for hours and tour information at [www.nps.gov/klgo].

E. Ketchikan

Welcome to Ketchikan, often the first stop for travellers entering Alaska's Inside Passage and famously known as the "Salmon Capital of the World" and "Totem Pole Capital of the World." This charming waterfront town, nestled between mountains and sea, is rich in indigenous culture, history, and outdoor beauty. From colourful totem poles to world-class fishing, Ketchikan offers a little bit of everything that makes Alaska unique.

Where It's Located and a Bit of History

Ketchikan is located on Revillagigedo Island in southeastern Alaska, positioned at the entrance of the Inside Passage. Founded in the late 1800s as a salmon cannery town, Ketchikan grew quickly as Alaska's fishing industry boomed. Today, the town is known for its vibrant Native heritage, with the largest collection of standing totem poles in the world, and its thriving arts scene. Ketchikan's fascinating blend of history and culture makes it a must-visit for anyone exploring Alaska.

Getting There

Most visitors arrive in Ketchikan by cruise ship, as it's a popular stop on Inside Passage itineraries. If you're flying in, Ketchikan International Airport (KTN) has regular flights from Seattle, as well as other Alaskan cities. From the airport, you'll take a short ferry ride across Tongass Narrows to reach the main town. Another option is the Alaska Marine Highway ferry system, which connects Ketchikan to other Southeast Alaska communities.

What to Do in Ketchikan

- Explore Totem Bight State Historical Park: Totem Bight is a beautiful park where you can walk among towering totem poles and learn about the traditions of Alaska's indigenous people. The park features 14 totem poles and a replica of a traditional Tlingit clan house, set against a stunning forested backdrop. Admission is free, and it's open year-round, though guided tours are usually available during the summer.

- <u>Stroll Down Creek Street:</u> Once the red-light district during Ketchikan's early days, Creek Street is now a charming boardwalk lined with shops, galleries, and museums. Take a leisurely walk along this historic waterfront and pop into places like Dolly's House Museum, where you can learn about the area's colorful past. Summer is prime time, as the creek fills with salmon, and you might even spot sea lions or eagles hunting nearby.

- <u>Go on a Fishing Adventure:</u> Ketchikan's nickname as the "Salmon Capital of the World" says it all – this is a top spot for fishing! Join a fishing charter for a chance to catch king salmon, halibut, or other local fish. Most fishing trips range from $150 to $300 per person, depending on the season and type of charter. If you're not into fishing, you can still visit the Ketchikan Fish Hatchery & Eagle Center to learn about the life cycle of salmon.

Where to Stay

Ketchikan has a range of accommodations, from cosy inns to waterside lodges:

- Cape Fox Lodge: Perched on a hill with views over the harbour, Cape Fox Lodge combines comfort with scenic views. Rooms start around $200 per night. Book your stay at [www.capefoxlodge.com].

- The Landing Hotel: Located near the airport ferry terminal, this hotel is convenient for travellers and offers a friendly, homey atmosphere. Rooms here start around $180 per night. Reserve a room at www.landinghotel.com.

- Black Bear Inn: For a more personal touch, this charming B&B offers waterfront views and cosy rooms starting at $160 per night. You can book directly at [www.stayinalaska.com].

Where to Eat and Drink

Ketchikan's food scene is all about fresh seafood and local flavours. Here are some must-visit spots:

- Alaska Fish House: Known for its fish and chips and smoked salmon chowder, this spot is a favourite among visitors and locals. A meal here will cost around $15-$20 per person. Check out more at [www.alaskafishhouse.com].

- Annabelle's Famous Keg & Chowder House: Located in the historic Gilmore Hotel, Annabelle's serves Alaskan seafood with a cosy, vintage vibe. Try the king crab legs or seafood chowder. A meal for two typically costs around $60. Visit [www.annabellesketchikan.com] for details.

- Sweet Mermaids: This charming café is great for breakfast or a light lunch, offering dishes like salmon benedicts and homemade pastries. A meal here is about $10-$15. They're located right on Front Street, so it's easy to stop by as you explore.

Best Time to Visit

The best time to visit Ketchikan is during the summer months, from May to September, when temperatures are mild (around 50-65°F) and the days are long. Summer is also when you'll have the best chances for activities like fishing and wildlife viewing, and when the town's festivals and events are in full swing. Keep in mind that Ketchikan is one of the rainiest places in the U.S., so bring rain gear no matter the season!

Useful Contacts

- Ketchikan Visitor Information Center: Located at 131 Front Street, open daily during cruise season. Call (907) 225-6166 or visit [www.visit-ketchikan.com].
- Alaska Marine Highway: For ferry schedules and information, visit [www.dot.alaska.gov/amhs].
- Ketchikan International Airport: Visit [www.borough.ketchikan.ak.us/air] or call (907) 225-6800 for flight information.

F. Denali National Park

Welcome to Denali National Park, home to North America's tallest peak, Denali, and one of the most awe-inspiring wilderness areas in the world. Imagine a place where the mountains touch the sky, where grizzly bears roam freely, and where the vast, untouched landscapes make you feel like you're truly on the edge of the wild. Whether you're here for adventure, wildlife, or simply to breathe in Alaska's natural beauty, Denali promises an unforgettable experience.

Where It's Located and a Bit of History

Denali National Park and Preserve is located in central Alaska, about 240 miles north of Anchorage and 125 miles south of Fairbanks. Established as Mount McKinley National Park in 1917, it was later renamed Denali, a nod to the indigenous Athabaskan word meaning "The Great One." Covering over six million acres, Denali is a true wilderness with a single road running through it, allowing visitors a rare chance to explore Alaska's wild beauty while preserving the natural habitat.

How to Get There

You can reach Denali National Park by car, train, or bus. If you're driving, take the Parks Highway (AK-3) from Anchorage or Fairbanks, which offers a scenic 4-5 hour drive from either city. The Alaska Railroad also runs a Denali Star Train from both cities during the summer, a journey that's almost as breathtaking as the park itself. Shuttle buses are another option, with several companies offering trips from Anchorage and Fairbanks directly to the park.

What to Do in Denali

- Take a Bus Tour into the Park: Since private vehicles aren't allowed beyond Mile 15 on the park road, a bus tour is the best way to explore Denali. The park offers several bus options, from narrated tours to simple hop-on, hop-off shuttles. The Tundra Wilderness Tour, for example, is a 7-8 hour trip that takes you deep into the park, with chances to spot wildlife and enjoy scenic stops. Tickets start around $140 per adult, and it's best to book early through [www.reservedenali.com].

- Go Wildlife Spotting: Denali is famous for its wildlife, and with luck, you'll spot some of the park's "Big Five": grizzly bears, wolves, moose, Dall sheep, and caribou. Other common sightings include foxes, golden eagles, and if you're lucky, even a wolverine! Bring binoculars, and keep your eyes peeled from your bus seat or from trails closer to the entrance.

- Hiking and Exploring Trails: While Denali is mostly trail-less to protect its wild environment, the front part of the park offers several marked trails for all fitness levels. Try the Horseshoe Lake Trail for an easy, scenic hike along a beautiful lake, or the Savage River Loop Trail, a moderate 2-mile loop with views of mountains and river valleys. Be sure to carry bear spray and always check trail conditions with the rangers.

Where to Stay

Accommodation options in Denali range from lodges and cabins near the park entrance to camping within the park itself:

- Denali Bluffs Hotel: Located just outside the park, this hotel offers stunning views, comfortable rooms, and easy access to park activities. Rates start at around $250 per night. Book through [www.denalialaska.com].

- McKinley Chalet Resort: Set along the Nenana River, this resort has cozy cabins and lovely views, perfect for those who want a blend of comfort and nature. Rates start around $200 per night. Reservations can be made at [www.mckinleychaletrresort.com].

- Camping in Denali: For a more rugged experience, consider camping at one of the park's six campgrounds. Riley Creek Campground near the entrance is a popular choice, with sites starting around $20 per night. You can book sites online at [www.recreation.gov].

Where to Eat and Drink

Denali's dining options are concentrated around the park entrance area:

- 49th State Brewing Co.: Located in nearby Healy, this brewery serves up hearty Alaskan fare like elk burgers and smoked salmon chowder, along with a selection of craft beers. Meals for two cost around $50. Find more at [www.49thstatebrewing.com].

- Denali Park Salmon Bake: Known locally as "The Bake," this spot serves fresh Alaskan salmon, halibut, and hearty comfort food in a casual, rustic setting. A meal here costs around $20 per person. Learn more at [www.denaliparksalmonbake.com].

- Panorama Pizza Pub: If you're craving a pizza night, this casual pub offers hand-tossed pizzas and views of the mountains. Expect to spend around $15-$20 per person. No website, but you'll find it easily along the park's entrance road.

Best Time to Visit

The best time to visit Denali is from late May to early September. Summer brings mild temperatures (50-70°F), long daylight hours, and most park services and accommodations are open. If you're interested in fall colors, early September is stunning but brings cooler temperatures and limited services as the season winds down. Winter visits are possible, but only for the adventurous, as temperatures can drop well below zero, and much of the park road is closed to vehicles.

Useful Contacts

- Denali Visitor Center: Located at the park entrance, open daily from mid-May to mid-September. Call (907) 683-9532 or visit [www.nps.gov/dena].
- Alaska Railroad: For train schedules and tickets, visit [www.alaskarailroad.com] or call (907) 265-2494.
- Denali Bus Tours: For tour reservations, visit [www.reservedenali.com] or call (800) 622-7275.

Chapter 4: Itinerary Planning for Tourists

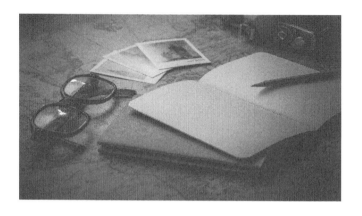

A. 3-Day, 7-Day, and 14-Day Options

3-Day Itinerary: Highlights of Anchorage and Denali

If you have only three days, focus on experiencing Anchorage and a taste of Denali National Park. Here's how to make the most of a short visit:

Day 1: Explore Anchorage
- Start your day with a visit to the Anchorage Museum to get an introduction to Alaska's history and indigenous culture.

- Head to the Alaska Native Heritage Center for performances, traditional crafts, and exhibits that highlight Alaska's rich indigenous heritage.
- End the day at Tony Knowles Coastal Trail for a scenic bike ride or walk along the coast with views of the Chugach Mountains and, if you're lucky, local wildlife like moose.

Day 2: Road Trip to Denali
- Take an early morning drive or scenic Alaska Railroad train ride to Denali National Park.
- Spend the afternoon on a Denali bus tour to spot wildlife, admire breathtaking views, and learn about the park's unique ecosystem.
- Stay overnight near the park entrance, ready for more adventure the next day.

Day 3: Denali Adventure
- In the morning, go on a short hike around the entrance trails or take a flightseeing tour for an aerial view of Denali's towering peaks.
- Drive or take the train back to Anchorage in the late afternoon or evening.

7-Day Itinerary: Anchorage, Seward, and Denali

With a week, you can explore the highlights of Anchorage, experience Denali, and add a visit to the stunning coastal town of Seward.

Day 1-2: Discover Anchorage
Spend your first two days as outlined in the 3-day itinerary, visiting Anchorage's top sights and immersing yourself in Alaskan culture.

Day 3-4: Denali National Park
- Follow the same route to Denali, with a full day dedicated to exploring the park via a bus tour and short hikes.
- Stay an extra night near Denali to fully experience the area's beauty.

Day 5: Travel to Seward
- Take the scenic drive from Anchorage to Seward along the Seward Highway, one of Alaska's most beautiful road trips.
- Arrive in Seward and explore the small town, visit the Alaska SeaLife Center, and enjoy dinner overlooking Resurrection Bay.

Day 6: Kenai Fjords National Park
- Spend the day on a Kenai Fjords boat tour, where you'll see glaciers, spot sea lions, otters, whales, and enjoy stunning coastal scenery.
- Spend another night in Seward or return to Anchorage in the evening.

Day 7: Back to Anchorage
- Take the scenic drive back to Anchorage, stopping along the way to see sites like Portage Glacier or to go on a short hike.
- Spend your final evening in Anchorage for a last taste of Alaskan cuisine.

14-Day Itinerary: A Grand Alaska Adventure

With two weeks, you'll have the chance to experience more of Alaska's diverse landscapes and culture, including Fairbanks, Juneau, and additional outdoor adventures.

Days 1-3: Anchorage and Denali
- Spend your first few days as in the 7-day itinerary, enjoying Anchorage and the best of Denali National Park.

Days 4-5: Fairbanks and Arctic Adventure
- Head north to Fairbanks, where you can explore the Museum of the North and try local foods.
- Book a tour to the Arctic Circle or take an evening aurora viewing tour if you're visiting in the fall or winter months.

Days 6-7: Back to Anchorage and Prepare for the Inside Passage
- Return to Anchorage, then prepare for a journey to Southeast Alaska's Inside Passage, either by a quick flight or a scenic ferry.

Days 8-10: Juneau and Glacier Bay

- Fly to Juneau, Alaska's capital, where you can visit Mendenhall Glacier, take the Mount Roberts Tramway, and explore local shops.
- Take a day trip to Glacier Bay National Park, known for its dramatic glaciers and abundant marine life.

Days 11-12: Ketchikan and Totem Bight

- Take the ferry or a short flight to Ketchikan, the "Salmon Capital of the World." Visit Totem Bight State Historical Park to see the world's largest collection of standing totem poles.
- Walk along Creek Street, once Ketchikan's historic red-light district, and enjoy some fresh seafood.

Days 13-14: Seward and Kenai Fjords National Park

- Finish your trip in Seward, spending a day exploring Kenai Fjords, where you'll get to see incredible glaciers, marine wildlife, and Alaska's coastal beauty.
- Return to Anchorage to wrap up your Alaskan journey with a final night in the city.

B. Customising Your Journey Based on Interest: Wildlife, Adventure, and Culture

Here's how to tailor your trip to match your passions. Let's explore some options to make sure your Alaskan journey is everything you're hoping for.

For Wildlife Lovers

If spotting Alaska's famous wildlife is your main goal, here are some unforgettable options:

- Denali National Park: Denali is known for its "Big Five" wildlife – grizzly bears, moose, wolves, caribou, and Dall sheep. Take a guided bus tour deep into the park for your best chance at seeing these amazing creatures in their natural habitat.

- Katmai National Park (Brooks Falls): Katmai is a paradise for bear watchers. Head to Brooks Falls during July, when brown bears gather to fish for salmon. You can view these majestic animals from a safe platform, giving you an up-close look without disturbing them.

- Kenai Fjords National Park: A boat tour through Kenai Fjords offers plenty of wildlife sightings, from sea otters and sea lions to orcas and humpback whales. Look out for puffins and other seabirds along the coastline as well.

For Adventure Seekers

Alaska is an adventure lover's playground, with endless opportunities for thrilling outdoor activities:

- Glacier Hiking and Ice Climbing: Matanuska Glacier, about two hours from Anchorage, offers accessible glacier hiking and even ice climbing. Guided tours let you explore the fascinating blue ice formations and deep crevasses safely.

- Whitewater Rafting: Head to Six Mile Creek or Nenana River near Denali for an adrenaline-filled rafting experience. Six Mile Creek, known for its exciting Class IV and V rapids, is ideal for seasoned adventurers, while Nenana River has options for both beginners and experienced rafters.

- Flightseeing and Mountaineering on Denali: For a truly thrilling experience, take a flightseeing tour around Denali, or if you're an experienced climber, consider a mountaineering expedition. Seeing Denali's peaks from the sky or up close is an unforgettable adventure.

For Culture and History Buffs

For those drawn to Alaska's rich history and cultural heritage, there are countless ways to explore:

- Alaska Native Heritage Center (Anchorage): Dive into Alaska's indigenous cultures at this immersive center. Through live performances, native storytelling, and exhibits on traditional crafts, you'll get an authentic look into the lives and history of Alaska's native peoples.

- Historic Skagway: Step back into the gold rush days with a visit to Skagway. This town feels like a living museum, with wooden boardwalks, historic saloons, and gold rush artifacts. Don't miss the Klondike Gold Rush National Historical Park, where you can even pan for gold.

- Totem Bight State Historical Park (Ketchikan): This park is home to one of the largest collections of totem poles, each with unique carvings telling the stories of indigenous Alaskan clans. Walk through the park's trails to see traditional totem poles and learn about the meanings behind them.

Tips for Customizing Your Trip

1. Mix and Match: Alaska's destinations often combine several interests. For example, you can go whale watching in Kenai Fjords National Park and also explore glaciers and kayak – it's all in one place!

2. Check Local Events: Alaska hosts cultural festivals, native gatherings, and art fairs throughout the year. Check ahead to see if any events align with your travel dates for an added cultural experience.

3. Consider a Guided Tour: Many outfitters offer specialized tours based on interests, from birdwatching expeditions to gold panning adventures, ensuring you see Alaska through the lens of what excites you most.

Chapter 5: Outdoor Adventures

A. Hiking and Camping

Imagine waking up in the heart of Alaska, surrounded by towering mountains, endless forests, and crisp, fresh air. Alaska's hiking and camping opportunities offer the best way to experience this incredible landscape, and the best part? You don't need to pay a thing to enjoy much of it. Alaska's public lands are open to everyone, and many of the state's beautiful trails and camping areas are free to explore. Here's your guide to making the most of Alaska's trails and campsites without breaking the bank.

Top Free Hiking Spots in Alaska

- Flattop Mountain (Anchorage): Just a short drive from downtown Anchorage, Flattop Mountain is one of Alaska's most popular hikes, and it's free! This 3-mile round-trip trail gives you incredible panoramic views of the city, Cook Inlet, and the Chugach Mountains. If you're up for it, the final ascent to the top has some rocky sections that add a bit of adventure. On a clear day, you can even catch a glimpse of Denali in the distance.

- <u>Savage River Loop (Denali National Park)</u>: You don't need a ticket or guide to enjoy the beauty of Denali! The Savage River Loop is a 2-mile, easy trail that follows the river and gives you a chance to spot local wildlife, like Dall sheep and even the occasional moose. It's one of the best free activities in Denali National Park, and the trail's gentle terrain makes it perfect for everyone, including families and beginners.

- <u>Byron Glacier Trail (Portage Valley)</u>: This gentle trail leads you right to the foot of Byron Glacier, where you can walk along the ice and even touch it! The trail is about 1.4 miles each way, making it accessible and family-friendly. Bring layers, as it gets chilly near the glacier, and don't forget your camera for some amazing photo opportunities.

Free Camping in Alaska's Public Lands

One of the great things about Alaska is that much of the state's vast wilderness is free to camp on. With public lands managed by the Bureau of Land Management (BLM) and the U.S. Forest Service, there are plenty of spots where you can set up camp without paying a fee.

- Denali National Park: Riley Creek Campground, located near the park entrance, is free in the off-season (mid-September to mid-May), giving you a budget-friendly option to camp at one of the most iconic places in Alaska. While you won't find services like showers in the off-season, the experience of camping near Denali's wilderness makes it all worth it.

- Chugach National Forest: If you're looking for a peaceful camping spot close to Anchorage, Chugach National Forest offers free dispersed camping options. This means you can camp almost anywhere in the forest, giving you endless possibilities. Just make sure to follow Leave No Trace principles, pack out all your waste, and camp at least 100 feet away from water sources.

- BLM Land near Kenai Peninsula: The Kenai Peninsula is an adventurer's paradise, and there's plenty of BLM land where you can camp for free. Explore nearby lakes, trails, and fishing spots, and enjoy the freedom of setting up camp wherever you find a beautiful spot.

Tips for a Safe and Enjoyable Free Camping Experience

1. Stay Bear Aware: Alaska is bear country, so keep all food in bear-proof containers, and cook at least 100 feet from where you sleep. Making noise while hiking is also a good way to avoid surprising any wildlife.

2. Dress for All Weather: Even in summer, Alaska's weather can be unpredictable. Dress in layers, and bring a waterproof jacket and sturdy hiking boots. Mornings and evenings can be chilly, so pack a hat and gloves, too.

3. Plan Ahead for Dispersed Camping: Dispersed camping means camping outside of developed campsites, so you'll need to be self-sufficient. Bring all the gear you'll need, including a water filter, since you might not have access to facilities.

4. Practice Leave No Trace: Alaska's natural beauty is something special, and it's up to all of us to keep it that way. Carry out all trash, avoid disturbing wildlife, and stick to marked trails whenever possible. This ensures that the land remains pristine for future generations.

B. Wildlife Viewing

Alaska is one of the world's best destinations for wildlife lovers, offering a rare chance to see majestic animals in their natural habitats. Here's how you can make the most of wildlife viewing without spending a dime.

Best Places for Free Wildlife Viewing

- Denali National Park: Denali is famous for its "Big Five" – grizzly bears, wolves, moose, caribou, and Dall sheep. You don't need a ticket to explore Denali's open areas or take short hikes along the Savage River Loop, where you're likely to spot wildlife. The Denali Park Road offers incredible viewing opportunities, especially early in the morning or late in the evening when animals are most active.

- Turnagain Arm (near Anchorage): If you're driving along the Seward Highway, the stretch known as Turnagain Arm is one of the best places for spotting wildlife. Keep your eyes peeled for Dall sheep on the mountainsides, beluga whales in the inlet (especially in late summer), and even black bears grazing along the roadsides. There are plenty of pull-outs where you can safely stop to take in the views.

- Potter Marsh (Anchorage): Just south of Anchorage, Potter Marsh is a free, family-friendly spot with boardwalks that take you right into the heart of an active wildlife area. It's a popular nesting spot for migratory birds, including sandhill cranes and trumpeter swans, and you may even spot a moose grazing nearby. The best time to visit is in the early morning or late afternoon when animals are most active.

Seasonal Tips for Wildlife Viewing

- Spring and Early Summer (May to June): Spring is a fantastic time to spot baby animals, as many species, including moose and caribou, give birth during this period. Migratory birds also begin to arrive, and you can enjoy spotting them across Alaska's many marshes and coastal areas.

- Late Summer (July to August): Salmon runs bring bears to rivers and streams across Alaska, with popular viewing spots like Brooks Falls in Katmai (accessible for free if you're able to make it to the area). Look for bald eagles gathering near rivers where salmon are plentiful.

- <u>Fall (September):</u> As the weather cools, caribou and moose begin their rutting season, making them more active and easier to spot. It's also a beautiful time for wildlife photography, with Alaska's autumn colours providing a vibrant backdrop.

Staying Safe While Watching Wildlife

<u>1. Keep Your Distance:</u> It's tempting to get close, but remember that Alaska's animals are wild and unpredictable. Always keep a safe distance—at least 100 yards from bears and 25 yards from other animals.

<u>2. Bring Binoculars:</u> Alaska's vast landscapes mean animals are often far away. A good pair of binoculars will help you observe wildlife up close without disturbing them.

<u>3. Be Bear Aware:</u> When hiking in bear country, make noise to alert any animals to your presence. If you're carrying food, pack it in bear-proof containers, and always dispose of waste properly.

C. Fishing and Hunting

If you're looking to experience Alaska like a local, there's no better way than fishing and hunting. Alaska offers an abundance of both activities, from casting for salmon in crystal-clear rivers to hunting for caribou in remote backcountry areas. These activities are more than just pastimes here—they're a part of life, tradition, and survival. If you're excited to join in, here's everything you need to know to make your Alaskan fishing or hunting adventure unforgettable.

Fishing in Alaska:

Alaska's rivers, lakes, and coastal waters are some of the best places in the world for fishing. Whether you're an experienced angler or a beginner, there's something here for everyone.

- <u>Salmon Fishing:</u> Alaska is known for its salmon runs, which take place throughout the summer. You can find different species, including king, sockeye, and coho salmon, in rivers and coastal areas from May through September. The Kenai River, Russian River, and Copper River are all famous spots, with peak season in July. For a chance to experience the thrill of reeling in a big catch, all you need is a fishing license, available online or at local stores.

- Halibut Fishing: Halibut is another Alaskan favourite, and these massive flatfish are usually found in deeper waters. Popular halibut fishing spots include Homer (the "Halibut Fishing Capital of the World"), Seward, and the waters around Kodiak Island. Many local charters offer half-day or full-day trips, providing gear and guidance for a great experience. Halibut season typically runs from mid-May to mid-September.

- Trout and Char Fishing: For those who prefer freshwater fishing, Alaska's streams and lakes are full of rainbow trout, Arctic char, and Dolly Varden. These species are fun to catch and offer plenty of spots for peaceful fishing in beautiful settings. Try your luck at the Brooks River or Quartz Lake, and enjoy the tranquility Alaska's interior has to offer.

Hunting in Alaska:

Hunting in Alaska is both a challenging adventure and a way to connect deeply with the land. Alaskan hunting is unique because it's rooted in tradition, sustenance, and respect for nature. Whether you're interested in big game or small game hunting, Alaska offers an unforgettable experience.

- <u>Big Game Hunting (Moose, Caribou, and Bear)</u>: Alaska's big game is famous worldwide. Moose and caribou are sought-after species, and each requires careful planning, as many hunting areas are remote and accessible only by plane or boat. If you're hunting brown or black bear, note that guided hunting is often required for non-residents. This ensures safety, ethical practices, and respect for the ecosystem. Hunting seasons vary by species and area, so check the Alaska Department of Fish and Game's website for specific dates.

- <u>Small Game Hunting</u>: For those interested in small game, Alaska offers grouse, ptarmigan, snowshoe hare, and more. Small game hunting is often less intensive, requiring minimal equipment and easy access to hunting grounds. This makes it a good option for those who want a simpler experience that still connects them to Alaska's wild bounty.

Licensing and Regulations

To participate in fishing and hunting in Alaska, you'll need the appropriate licenses and permits. Non-residents can purchase licenses online or at various stores across the state. Here are some things to keep in mind:

1. Fishing License: A one-day license starts around $15, and multi-day options are available. Additional permits may be required for king salmon fishing.

2. Hunting License: Non-residents will need a hunting license, which varies in price depending on the species and duration. Big game hunting often requires additional tags, which can range from $150 to $1000 depending on the animal.

3. Follow Regulations Carefully: Alaska has strict regulations to maintain its ecosystem and protect wildlife. Make sure to review the rules on catch limits, hunting seasons, and restricted areas, as fines for violations are serious.

Responsible Fishing and Hunting

1. Practice "Catch and Release" When Possible: If you're fishing for sport, consider releasing your catch to maintain fish populations. Many Alaskan rivers have "catch and release" policies for certain species, so check the guidelines for each location.

2. Dispose of Waste Properly: Alaska's wilderness is pristine, and it's important to keep it that way. Pack out everything you bring in, especially fish waste and food scraps, to avoid attracting wildlife to campgrounds or fishing spots.

3. Respect Animal Populations: Only hunt what you intend to use, and avoid overfishing or overhunting. Alaska's resources are here for everyone, and practicing respectful, sustainable hunting and fishing helps preserve them for future generations.

D. Winter Sports and Activities

If you're visiting Alaska in winter, you're in for a real treat. Alaska transforms into a snowy wonderland from November through March, offering endless opportunities for outdoor fun and adventure. Whether you're looking to ski down powdery slopes, explore the wilderness on a snowmobile, or watch the magical northern lights, Alaska has it all. Here's how you can dive into the best winter activities Alaska has to offer.

1. Skiing and Snowboarding

Alaska's mountains are legendary for their beauty and challenge, making it a paradise for skiing and snowboarding enthusiasts. Here are some top spots:

- **Alyeska Resort (Girdwood):** Just 40 miles from Anchorage, Alyeska Resort is Alaska's premier ski destination. It has over 1,600 skiable acres, with slopes for all skill levels. Whether you're a beginner or an expert, you'll find runs that suit your style, along with breathtaking views of the Chugach Mountains. Daily lift tickets are around $60-$95, with rentals and lessons available for those new to the sport.

- **Eaglecrest Ski Area (Juneau):** Eaglecrest, located just outside Juneau, offers 640 acres of slopes and is known for its friendly, laid-back vibe. It's a great spot for families and beginners, with reasonable lift ticket prices starting at $35 for half-day passes. Plus, you'll get the chance to ski with locals and enjoy stunning views of Gastineau Channel.

2. Dog Sledding

Dog sledding is a unique way to experience Alaska's winter and get a taste of its heritage. Many Alaskan communities have dog sledding tours and trails where you can hop on a sled and ride through snow-covered forests and mountains.

- Denali National Park Dog Sled Tours: In winter, you can book a dog sled tour in Denali to experience the thrill of mushing with a team of eager huskies. Tours vary in length, from short rides to full-day excursions, and some even offer the chance to learn basic mushing skills.

- Iditarod Trail Headquarters (Wasilla): If you're interested in the history of dog sledding, a visit to the Iditarod Trail Headquarters is a must. Here, you can learn about the iconic Iditarod race and meet some of the huskies who participate. Short rides are available, making it a fun stop for families.

3. Northern Lights Viewing

Winter in Alaska is prime time for viewing the northern lights. From Fairbanks to remote lodges, you'll find spots perfect for watching the aurora dance across the night sky.

- Fairbanks: Known as one of the best places in the world to see the northern lights, Fairbanks offers plenty of aurora viewing tours. Many lodges and hotels also have wake-up calls for guests when the aurora appears, so you won't miss a moment of the show.

- Coldfoot Camp (Gates of the Arctic): For a more rugged experience, Coldfoot Camp offers guided tours into the wilderness for aurora viewing. It's located right above the Arctic Circle, where your chances of seeing the lights are incredibly high. They even provide warm cabins, so you can stay comfortable between aurora sightings.

4. Snowmobiling

Snowmobiling is a thrilling way to explore Alaska's remote wilderness, allowing you to cover miles of snowy trails and enjoy landscapes that are often inaccessible in winter by other means.

- Anchorage Area Trails: Anchorage has several snowmobile rental services and guided tours for beginners and experienced riders. You can explore trails in the Chugach State Park, with scenic routes through frozen lakes and snow-dusted forests.

- Paxson and Eureka: These are popular areas for snowmobiling enthusiasts, with hundreds of miles of groomed trails through stunning backcountry. Local outfitters provide rentals and guided tours that allow you to enjoy the thrill of speed while surrounded by breathtaking landscapes.

5. Ice Fishing and Ice Climbing

For those looking for a more unique winter adventure, Alaska's icy landscapes offer both ice fishing and ice climbing.

- Ice Fishing on Big Lake or Lake Louise: Bundle up and experience ice fishing on Alaska's frozen lakes. Big Lake near Anchorage and Lake Louise in the interior are popular spots where locals and visitors alike gather to fish for trout, pike, and salmon. You'll need a fishing license, which you can purchase online, and ice fishing gear, which many outfitters rent out.

- Matanuska Glacier Ice Climbing: If you're up for a challenge, try ice climbing on Matanuska Glacier. Guided tours take you out onto the glacier, where you'll learn to scale frozen walls and explore icy caves. It's a workout and a thrilling adventure, and you'll get to experience Alaska's glacial beauty up close.

Essential Tips for a Safe and Enjoyable Winter Adventure

1. Dress for the Cold: Alaska's winter temperatures can be extreme, so layers are essential. Wear moisture-wicking base layers, insulating mid-layers, and waterproof outer layers. Don't forget gloves, a hat, and warm socks!

2. Plan Your Trip in Advance: Winter in Alaska can bring unexpected weather and road conditions, so plan ahead. Book tours and accommodations early, and always check the weather forecast.

3. Stay Safe and Be Aware of Wildlife: Winter wildlife like moose are more active near roads and trails. Keep your distance, stay aware, and always follow safety instructions provided by guides or locals.

Chapter 6: Alaska Cuisine and Dining

A. Must-Try Local Dishes

One of the best parts of any trip to Alaska is diving into the local cuisine, where fresh seafood, wild game, and indigenous ingredients come together in some seriously memorable dishes. Let's explore a few must-try dishes that'll give you a true taste of Alaska's culinary heart.

1. Wild Alaskan Salmon

Alaskan salmon isn't just any salmon—it's some of the freshest, most flavourful fish you'll ever taste. Whether it's served smoked, grilled, or in a rich chowder, wild-caught Alaskan salmon is a must. If you're here in the summer, you might even catch a taste of freshly-caught salmon at a riverside fish fry or a local restaurant that sources right from the sea. King, sockeye, and coho salmon are especially popular, each with its own unique flavour profile.

2. Alaskan King Crab

If you're a seafood lover, you'll want to try Alaskan king crab. Known for its tender, sweet meat and rich flavour, it's often served with just a touch of melted butter, allowing the freshness to shine through. King crab is typically available year-round but is especially popular in the colder months when the crabbing season is at its peak. Be sure to order it at least once while you're here—whether it's a casual spot or a fine dining restaurant, this dish never disappoints.

3. Reindeer Sausage

A uniquely Alaskan dish, reindeer sausage has a smoky, savoury taste with a hint of spice. You'll find it on breakfast menus, in hot dogs, and even on pizza! Locals enjoy it grilled, with a side of mustard or in a warm bun with all the fixings. It's a hearty, flavourful snack that captures Alaska's wild side and is a great option for a quick bite on the go.

4. Halibut Fish and Chips

Alaskan halibut is another seafood staple with a mild, buttery flavour. One of the best ways to enjoy it? Halibut fish and chips! This dish is crispy, golden, and satisfying, often served with a side of tartar sauce and a wedge of lemon. You'll find it on menus across Alaska, especially in coastal towns where the fish is fresh from the sea.

5. Akutaq (Eskimo Ice Cream)

If you're up for trying something totally unique, give Akutaq a go. Known as "Eskimo ice cream," this traditional native dish is a blend of whipped animal fat, wild berries, and sometimes fish or reindeer. While that may sound unusual, it's a beloved treat in Alaska's native communities. Many modern versions use vegetable shortening and sugar, so you can experience a taste of tradition with a contemporary twist.

6. Alaskan Blueberry and Birch Syrup Treats

Alaskan blueberries are a summer favourite, with a flavour that's rich and a little tart. You'll find these berries in everything from pies and jams to sauces and syrups. And if you have a sweet tooth, don't miss birch syrup—it's similar to maple syrup but has a uniquely earthy flavour. Birch syrup is often drizzled over pancakes, salmon, or desserts, adding a taste of the Alaskan forest to your meal.

7. Caribou Stew

For a true taste of Alaska's wilderness, try a bowl of caribou stew. This hearty dish often includes chunks of tender caribou meat, potatoes, carrots, and a mix of herbs and spices. It's a warming, filling meal perfect for cooler days, and many locals see it as comfort food that celebrates Alaska's hunting traditions.

8. Sourdough Bread

Alaska has a long history with sourdough, dating back to the gold rush era when miners relied on sourdough starters to make bread in the wilderness. Today, you'll find sourdough everywhere, from bakeries to breakfast spots. With its tangy flavour and rustic texture, Alaskan sourdough is the perfect addition to any meal or a tasty snack on its own.

Where to Find These Dishes

You'll discover these iconic dishes across Alaska, from casual eateries to upscale restaurants. Some local spots even feature seasonal menus, ensuring that what you're eating is as fresh as possible. Be sure to check out seafood markets in towns like Anchorage, Juneau, and Ketchikan, where you can buy fresh-caught fish and seafood to try yourself or take home.

B. Best Restaurants and Food Markets

Let's take a look at some must-visit restaurants and food markets to make sure you're getting the most out of your Alaskan food adventure.

Top Restaurants to Try

Simon & Seaforts Saloon & Grill (Anchorage)

Simon & Seaforts, known locally as "Simon's," is an Anchorage classic, serving up amazing seafood and incredible views of the Cook Inlet. Their king crab legs and grilled halibut are crowd favourites, and if you're in the mood for something indulgent, try their famous "seafort stuffed halibut" with crab stuffing and lemon butter. The restaurant is ideal for a nice dinner, with mains averaging around $30-$50. Reservations are recommended, especially during the summer.

Tracy's King Crab Shack (Juneau)

This casual spot in Juneau is all about fresh, no-frills seafood and is an absolute must for crab lovers. Tracy's King Crab Shack serves some of the best crab legs, crab cakes, and crab bisque you'll ever taste. Tracy's is all about authenticity, with outdoor seating and a laid-back atmosphere that captures the spirit of Alaska. Expect to spend around $25-$50 for a hearty, seafood-filled meal.

The Saltry Restaurant (Halibut Cove)

If you're looking for a unique dining experience, The Saltry in Halibut Cove is one of Alaska's most scenic and charming spots. Accessible only by boat from Homer, The Saltry serves seasonal, locally-sourced dishes like Alaskan salmon, halibut, and mussels, all with a creative twist. The food is delicious, the views are unbeatable, and the experience feels truly Alaskan. Mains are around $25-$45, and reservations are highly recommended.

Skagway Brewing Company (Skagway)

This cosy spot in Skagway is known for its craft beers made with local spruce tips and a hearty pub menu that includes reindeer sausage, fish and chips, and burgers. The spruce tip ale is a favourite, giving you a unique taste of Alaska's wild forests. Skagway Brewing Company is casual and fun, with meals averaging around $20-$30, and is a perfect stop after exploring the town.

Local Food Markets

Anchorage Market & Festival (Anchorage)

The Anchorage Market & Festival is held every weekend from May to September and is a lively spot to try Alaskan street food, buy local produce, and browse unique crafts. You'll find food vendors selling everything from reindeer sausages to freshly baked sourdough bread. It's a great way to try local flavours and pick up some Alaskan goodies to take home.

Juneau's Foodland IGA (Juneau)

This may sound like a regular grocery store, but Foodland IGA in Juneau has an excellent seafood selection, including fresh Alaskan salmon, halibut, and crab. They often carry local produce and have an in-store deli where you can grab ready-made dishes like smoked salmon and local cheeses. If you're staying in town for a while, it's a convenient spot to stock up on fresh, local ingredients.

Kodiak Island Seafood and Fish Market (Kodiak)

If you're visiting Kodiak, check out this local seafood market for fresh-caught fish and shellfish. The Kodiak Island Seafood and Fish Market sells wild-caught salmon, halibut, crab, and even seaweed products. It's perfect if you're planning to cook some meals on your own or want to try smoked salmon that's prepared right on the island.

A Few More Local Favourites

- <u>49th State Brewing Co. (Anchorage & Denali):</u> Known for its craft beer and lively atmosphere, this spot serves Alaskan dishes like elk burgers, fish tacos, and smoked salmon chowder. Both locations have stunning outdoor seating, and the Anchorage location offers beautiful views of the city and mountains. Meals range from $20-$40.

- <u>Humpy's Great Alaskan Alehouse (Anchorage):</u> A local favourite, Humpy's is famous for its seafood and laid-back vibe. Try the halibut tacos, fish and chips, or their classic clam chowder. Meals are around $15-$30, making it a great spot for a casual dinner.

Tips for Dining Out in Alaska

<u>1. Reservations Are Key:</u> During the summer months, popular spots like Tracy's King Crab Shack and Simon & Seaforts can get very busy. If you have a must-visit place on your list, it's best to book ahead to avoid long waits.

<u>2. Seasonal Menus:</u> Many Alaskan restaurants adjust their menus based on what's available locally and seasonally, so you're always likely to find fresh ingredients. Summer is ideal for seafood, while winter may bring hearty game dishes and comfort food.

3. Embrace the Local Ingredients: Whether it's trying spruce tip ale, birch syrup, or fresh salmon, embracing local ingredients is the best way to get a taste of Alaska. Don't be afraid to try something new!

C. Tips for Enjoying Fresh, Local Seafood in Alaska

1. Know the Seasons for the Best Catch

Alaska's seafood scene follows the rhythms of the natural world, with different types of fish and shellfish peaking at different times. For example:

- Salmon season runs from May to September, with sockeye, king, and coho salmon being the most popular varieties.
- Halibut is typically available from mid-March to mid-November, with its mild flavour and tender texture making it perfect for grilling or pan-searing.
- Alaskan king crab season peaks in the winter, generally from October to January, though some restaurants serve it year-round.

Knowing what's in season can help you make the most of your seafood experience, ensuring you're getting the freshest options.

2. Try a Seafood Market or Fish Fry

For an authentic taste of Alaska, visit a local seafood market. In towns like Anchorage, Juneau, and Ketchikan, you'll find seafood markets offering everything from fresh salmon fillets to live crab. Some even have cooking stations where you can try samples or have your purchases prepared to eat on the spot.

If you're looking for a casual dining experience, check out a fish fry. These local spots serve up freshly fried fish and chips, often with halibut or cod caught right from Alaskan waters. It's a great way to enjoy a delicious meal without the formality of a sit-down restaurant.

3. Embrace the "Simple Is Better" Philosophy

When it comes to Alaskan seafood, less is often more. Chefs here understand that the natural flavours of fresh-caught seafood need little enhancement. Look for dishes that are simply grilled, baked, or steamed, with minimal seasoning—often just a touch of salt, lemon, or butter. This approach lets the delicate flavours of the fish or shellfish shine through, giving you a true taste of Alaska.

4. Be Adventurous with Local Specialities

Alaska has some unique seafood dishes that you won't find anywhere else, so don't be afraid to try something new! If you see reindeer sausage or smoked salmon on the menu, give it a go. Salmon jerky and pickled kelp are also local favourites that make for great snacks on the go. And if you're dining somewhere that offers sablefish (also known as black cod)** or Dungeness crab, seize the chance—both are delicious and highly regarded in Alaska's food culture.

5. Take a Fishing Tour and Cook Your Own Catch

One of the best ways to enjoy Alaska's seafood is to catch it yourself! Many towns offer fishing charters where you can fish for salmon or halibut under the guidance of a local expert. Some charters even have options for "catch and cook," where they'll help you prepare your catch right on the boat or back on shore. There's something truly special about enjoying a meal you've caught yourself, and it's an experience you'll remember long after you leave.

6. Look for Sustainable and Wild-Caught Labels

Alaska is known for its commitment to sustainable fishing practices, and most of the seafood you'll find here is wild-caught rather than farmed. Look for restaurants or markets that highlight sustainability, with labels like "Alaska Wild" or "Certified Sustainable Seafood." Not only does this ensure you're getting high-quality seafood, but you're also supporting

Alaska's conservation efforts, helping preserve this resource for generations to come.

7. Pair Your Seafood with Local Brews or Wines

Enhance your Alaskan seafood experience with a local craft beer or a carefully selected wine. Alaskan brewing companies offer unique options like spruce tip ale, which pairs beautifully with seafood dishes. For wine, a crisp white wine like chardonnay or sauvignon blanc is a classic choice, as it complements the natural flavours of fish and shellfish without overwhelming them.

8. Bring Some Seafood Home with You

If you fall in love with Alaskan seafood (which is likely!), many seafood markets and stores offer vacuum-sealed and flash-frozen options that are perfect for taking home. You can bring a taste of Alaska back to your kitchen, or even ship some to friends and family. Just check your airline's policies on transporting seafood or arrange for it to be shipped directly to your home.

Chapter 7:
Accommodation Options

A. Hotels and Lodges

Anchorage:

Anchorage, Alaska's largest city, has a variety of hotels that cater to all kinds of travelers, from families to solo adventurers:

1. Hotel Captain Cook

SCAN THE QR CODE

1. Open your device camera app.
2. Position the QR code in the camera frame.
3. Hold your phone steady.
4. Wait for the code to be recognized.
5. Once recognized, tap on the notification or follow the prompt to access the content or action associated with the Qr code

Located in downtown Anchorage, Hotel Captain Cook is a favourite for its luxury and prime location. This four-star hotel offers elegant rooms with mountain or city views, three restaurants, and even an athletic club. Rooms start around $250 per night. It's a wonderful option if you're looking to treat yourself to comfort and convenience, with attractions like the Anchorage Museum and Tony Knowles Coastal Trail nearby.

2. Aloft Anchorage Midtown

SCAN THE QR CODE

1. Open your device camera app.
2. Position the QR code in the camera frame.
3. Hold your phone steady.
4. Wait for the code to be recognized.
5. Once recognized, tap on the notification or follow the prompt to access the content or action associated with the Qr code

This new and modern hotel is a fun, stylish option with an urban vibe. With an on-site bar, a fitness centre, and rooms starting at around $150, it's perfect for those who want comfort with a dash of contemporary flair. Located in midtown, it's just a quick drive from downtown Anchorage and close to several shopping and dining options.

3. Inlet Tower Hotel & Suites

For budget-conscious travelers, Inlet Tower offers clean, comfortable rooms with a central location at affordable rates, starting at around $100 per night. The hotel provides free shuttles to downtown Anchorage and the airport, making it a convenient choice for travellers looking to explore on a budget.

Denali:

If you're visiting Denali National Park, staying nearby allows you to enjoy the beauty and wildlife right at your doorstep. Here are some of the best spots to rest near this iconic park:

1. Denali Bluffs Hotel

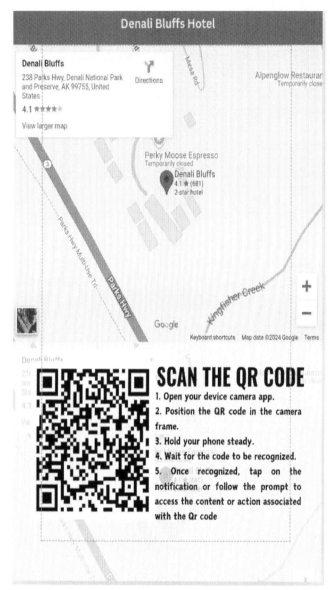

Just minutes from Denali's park entrance, Denali Bluffs Hotel is a charming lodge with rustic yet comfortable rooms, many offering views of the Nenana River. Room rates start around $200 per night. After a day of exploring the park, you can relax by the fire pit or enjoy Alaskan cuisine at the on-site restaurant, Mountaineer Grill & Bar.

2. Grande Denali Lodge

Grande Denali Lodge

Grande Denali Lodge

238 Parks Hwy, Denali National Park and Preserve, AK 99755, United States

Directions

4.0 ★★★★☆

View larger map

Grande Denali Lodge
4.0 ★ (553)
3-star hotel

Alpenglow Restaurant
Temporarily closed

Mesa Rd

Grande Rd

Kingfisher Creek

Google

Keyboard shortcuts   Map data ©2024 Google   Terms

SCAN THE QR CODE

1. Open your device camera app.
2. Position the QR code in the camera frame.
3. Hold your phone steady.
4. Wait for the code to be recognized.
5. Once recognized, tap on the notification or follow the prompt to access the content or action associated with the Qr code

Set high on Sugarloaf Mountain, Grande Denali Lodge gives you sweeping views of the Alaska Range and Denali National Park. Rooms start at about $250 per night, and the lodge has a warm, welcoming atmosphere with all the amenities you need, including an on-site restaurant. It's perfect for those seeking a mix of comfort and nature.

3. McKinley Creekside Cabins & Cafe

Located 13 miles south of the park entrance, McKinley Creekside Cabins offers a cozy, affordable stay with rates starting at around $150 per night. The on-site cafe serves fresh, locally-sourced meals, making it a fantastic choice if you're looking for a comfortable stay with a bit of rustic charm.

Juneau:

Juneau, Alaska's capital, is a picturesque town with unique hotels and lodges close to the sea and mountains.

1. Baranof Downtown Hotel

SCAN THE QR CODE

1. Open your device camera app.
2. Position the QR code in the camera frame.
3. Hold your phone steady.
4. Wait for the code to be recognized.
5. Once recognized, tap on the notification or follow the prompt to access the content or action associated with the Qr code

Located right in downtown Juneau, this historic hotel is one of the most popular stays in the capital. Rooms start around $170 per night and feature classic decor with modern touches. The hotel's location makes it easy to explore local attractions like the Alaska State Museum and Mendenhall Glacier.

2. Silverbow Inn & Suites

SCAN THE QR CODE

1. Open your device camera app.
2. Position the QR code in the camera frame.
3. Hold your phone steady.
4. Wait for the code to be recognized.
5. Once recognized, tap on the notification or follow the prompt to access the content or action associated with the Qr code

This boutique inn is a charming, modern choice in downtown Juneau. With complimentary breakfast, a rooftop hot tub, and rooms starting at around $160 per night, Silverbow Inn offers a cozy, intimate stay with a unique vibe.

3. Alaskan Hotel & Bar

For history buffs, the Alaskan Hotel & Bar, built in 1913, is Alaska's oldest operating hotel. Rooms start as low as $100 per night, offering a unique, old-world charm for budget travellers. Note that it's a historic building, so amenities are simpler, but it's full of character and located right in the heart of Juneau.

Seward:

Seward, located on the Kenai Peninsula, is a scenic town where you can enjoy coastal views and easy access to Kenai Fjords National Park.

1. Seward Windsong Lodge

Seward Windsong Lodge

Seward Windsong Lodge

31772 Herman Leirer Rd, Seward, AK
99664, United States

4.3 ★★★★★

View larger map

Directions

Seward Windsong Lodge
4.3 ★ (507)
3-star hotel

Google

Keyboard shortcuts Map data ©2024 Google Terms

SCAN THE QR CODE

1. Open your device camera app.

2. Position the QR code in the camera frame.

3. Hold your phone steady.

4. Wait for the code to be recognized.

5. Once recognized, tap on the notification or follow the prompt to access the content or action associated with the Qr code

Set in a peaceful forested area near Resurrection River, this lodge offers comfortable rooms with wilderness views. Rooms start around $200 per night, and the on-site Resurrection Roadhouse serves delicious Alaskan cuisine. It's ideal for nature lovers who want to experience Seward's rugged beauty with the comfort of a warm lodge.

2. Harbor 360 Hotel

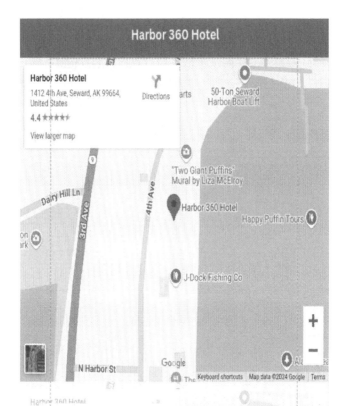

Harbor 360 Hotel

Harbor 360 Hotel
1412 4th Ave, Seward, AK 99664, United States
4.4 ★★★★★
View larger map

SCAN THE QR CODE

1. Open your device camera app.

2. Position the QR code in the camera frame.

3. Hold your phone steady.

4. Wait for the code to be recognized.

5. Once recognized, tap on the notification or follow the prompt to access the content or action associated with the Qr code

If you want to stay near the action, Harbor 360 Hotel, located right on the Seward Harbor, is a great choice. Rooms start around $150 per night, and the hotel offers beautiful views of the harbor and mountains, along with easy access to boat tours for whale watching and glacier cruises.

2. Breeze Inn Motel

For travelers on a budget, Breeze Inn Motel is a clean, comfortable choice near the small boat harbor. Rooms start at $100 per night, and the motel offers easy access to restaurants, shops, and Kenai Fjords tour departures.

Tips for Choosing Your Alaskan Stay

1. Book Early: Summer is peak season in Alaska, so it's wise to book your accommodations well in advance, especially in popular areas like Denali, Anchorage, and Seward.

2. Look for Local Amenities: Many lodges and hotels offer unique amenities, like on-site restaurants with local cuisine, shuttles to national parks, or activities like guided hikes and glacier tours.

3. Consider the Location: Staying close to your activities can make a big difference, especially when travelling long distances between destinations. Choose a location that keeps you close to the places you want to explore.

B. Camping and RV Parks

Camping Options in Alaska's National and State Parks

Alaska's national and state parks offer a variety of campsites for those who want to sleep under the stars surrounded by nature. Many of these parks provide both tent and RV camping options, with facilities ranging from basic to full-service.

- **Denali National Park (Riley Creek Campground)**: Located just inside Denali's park entrance, Riley Creek Campground is perfect for visitors exploring the park. It offers tent sites and RV parking, with fire pits, picnic tables, and flush toilets available. This campground is accessible year-round, and rates start at about $15 per night. Reservations are recommended during summer, and it's a great base for hiking and wildlife spotting.

- **Chugach State Park (Eagle River Campground)**: Just a short drive from Anchorage, Eagle River Campground in Chugach State Park is ideal for those looking to camp close to the city. It offers both tent sites and RV spots with access to toilets, water, and picnic areas. Set against a beautiful river backdrop, it's perfect for hiking, fishing, and watching wildlife. Rates start at $20 per night, and it's first-come, first-served, so arrive early to secure your spot.

- **Kenai Peninsula (Porcupine Campground, Hope):** Situated near the small town of Hope, Porcupine Campground overlooks Turnagain Arm, offering stunning coastal views and plenty of privacy. This campground is great for those who want a more secluded experience while still being close to fishing, hiking, and kayaking opportunities. Rates start around $15, and it's open from May to September. Porcupine is first-come, first-served, so try to get there early during peak season.

Popular RV Parks for Scenic Comfort

If you're exploring Alaska by RV, you'll find a number of well-equipped RV parks that provide not only a safe place to park but also stunning views and convenient amenities.

- **Seward Waterfront Park:** Located right on Resurrection Bay, Seward Waterfront Park offers RV parking with a view of the ocean and nearby mountains. It's close to downtown Seward and the boat harbor, making it convenient for exploring Kenai Fjords National Park. The RV park has both electric and non-electric sites, with rates starting around $20-$40 per night. It's popular in summer, so reservations are recommended.

- **Golden Nugget RV Park (Anchorage):** If you're visiting Anchorage, Golden Nugget RV Park is a great choice for RV travellers. This centrally located park has full hookups, laundry facilities, showers, and a small convenience store. It's close to Anchorage's main attractions, and rates start at around $40 per night. This is a good option for those looking for comfort and access to city amenities while exploring the surrounding wilderness.

- **Tok RV Village & Cabins (Tok):** Known as the "Gateway to Alaska," Tok is a common stop for those driving into Alaska from Canada. Tok RV Village offers spacious sites with full hookups, laundry, showers, and a cozy cabin-style lodge. Rates start at about $35 per night. It's a welcoming spot to rest up before or after your journey through the Alaskan wilderness.

C. Unique Stays

Cosy Cabins for Rustic Charm

Alaska's cabins are beloved by locals and visitors alike, offering warmth and comfort amid the wilderness. They're ideal for couples, families, or solo travellers who want an authentic Alaskan experience with a roof overhead.

- **Denali Backcountry Lodge (Denali National Park):** Deep within Denali, this remote lodge offers rustic cabins surrounded by incredible wilderness. Accessible only by bus, the lodge provides guided hikes, wildlife viewing, and meals, making it an all-inclusive experience in Alaska's backcountry. Rates start around $500 per night, including meals and activities, and it's best to book well in advance for summer stays.

- **Rustic Wilderness Cabins (Talkeetna):** Just outside the charming town of Talkeetna, these cabins offer an authentic Alaskan experience with cosy decor, kitchenettes, and easy access to outdoor activities. Rates start at around $150 per night. The cabins are close to Denali flightseeing tours, rafting, and other adventures, giving you a taste of small-town Alaska while staying comfortable.

- **Sven's Basecamp Hostel (Fairbanks):** For a budget-friendly and unique option, Sven's Basecamp offers log cabins and yurts with a rustic, adventurous vibe. Rates start at $80 per night, and you'll have access to a communal kitchen, shower facilities, and cozy common areas. It's a great spot for meeting other travellers and exploring Fairbanks' attractions.

Glamping

If you're excited to camp but prefer a touch of luxury, glamping is the way to go. Glamping in Alaska combines the thrill of sleeping close to nature with comfortable beds, warm blankets, and often private bathrooms.

- **Alpenglow Luxury Camping (Homer):** Located on the Kenai Peninsula with stunning views of Kachemak Bay, Alpenglow offers luxury canvas tents with real beds, cozy decor, and private decks. Each tent comes with a fire pit and heating for chilly nights, with rates starting at $150 per night. It's the perfect place to watch the sunset over the bay, surrounded by Alaska's wild beauty.

- **Under Canvas (Denali National Park):** Under Canvas offers a premier glamping experience just outside Denali National

Park. Their luxury tents come with king-size beds, wood stoves, and private bathrooms. Some tents even have viewing decks for starry nights or glimpses of the northern lights. Rates start at around $300 per night, and the location provides easy access to Denali's adventures while offering a unique blend of comfort and nature.

- **Orca Island Cabins (Seward):** Located on a private island in Resurrection Bay, these eco-friendly yurts provide an unforgettable glamping experience with stunning ocean views. Each yurt is fully furnished with beds, a kitchenette, and private decks overlooking the water. Rates start at $275 per night, including kayaks and paddleboards for exploring the bay. It's an ideal getaway for those who want peace, quiet, and a bit of adventure.

Unique, One-of-a-Kind Stays

For those looking for something truly special, Alaska offers unique accommodations that will make your stay unforgettable, from treehouses to lodges accessible only by boat or plane.

- **Treehouse Lodge (Ketchikan):** Ever dreamed of staying in a treehouse? This cozy lodge just outside Ketchikan lets you live out that fantasy. The lodge is surrounded by forest, with treehouses that offer beautiful views of the landscape and wildlife below. Rates start around $200 per night, making it a memorable experience for nature lovers.

- **Tutka Bay Lodge (Kenai Peninsula):** Accessible only by boat, Tutka Bay Lodge is a luxury retreat tucked away in a private fjord. It offers rustic-luxury cabins, gourmet dining, and activities like kayaking, hiking, and cooking classes. Rates start around $1,500 per night, all-inclusive. It's a splurge, but the secluded, beautiful setting is worth it for a once-in-a-lifetime experience.

- **Sheldon Chalet (Ruth Glacier, Denali):** If you're looking for ultimate exclusivity and breathtaking views, Sheldon Chalet on Ruth Glacier offers just that. Situated in the heart of Denali National Park, this luxurious chalet is accessible only by helicopter and offers five-star accommodations surrounded by glaciers. Rates start around $2,300 per person per night, including meals, guides, and helicopter access. This is truly a bucket-list experience for those who want something extraordinary.

Tips for Booking Unique Stays in Alaska

<u>1. Book Early for Summer Stays:</u> Summer is peak season in Alaska, so unique stays like glamping and cabins book up quickly. Planning several months in advance is highly recommended.

<u>2. Consider Off-Season Rates:</u> If you're open to cooler weather, Alaska's shoulder seasons (spring and fall) often offer lower rates and fewer crowds, making it a great time to book unique stays at a discount.

<u>3. Check for All-Inclusive Options:</u> Some lodges and remote stays offer all-inclusive packages that include meals, activities, and transportation. While these may seem pricey, they can be a great value for those wanting a hassle-free, adventure-packed experience.

Chapter 8:
Transportation Within Alaska

A. Renting a Car

Renting a car in Alaska offers the freedom to explore its vast landscapes at your own pace. Here's what you need to know:

Why Rent a Car in Alaska?

Alaska's expansive terrain and limited public transportation make car rentals a practical choice for travelers. With a rental car, you can access remote areas, scenic byways, and national parks that might be challenging to reach otherwise.

Major Car Rental Companies

In cities like Anchorage, Fairbanks, and Juneau, you'll find well-known rental agencies such as:

- Avis Alaska: Offers a range of vehicles suitable for Alaskan roads.

- Enterprise Rent-A-Car: Provides various options, including SUVs and trucks.

- Budget Car Rental: Known for competitive rates and multiple locations.

Local Car Rental Companies

Local agencies often provide vehicles tailored for Alaskan conditions:

- **Alaska 4x4 Rentals:** Specializes in four-wheel-drive vehicles, ideal for rugged terrains.

- Alaska Auto Rental: Offers a variety of vehicles with flexible rental terms.

Booking Tips

- Advance Reservations: During peak tourist season (June to August), demand is high. Booking several months in advance can secure better rates and vehicle availability. citeturn0search10

- <u>One-Way Rentals:</u> If planning a one-way trip, confirm with the rental company about drop-off locations and any additional fees.

Cost Considerations

Rental prices vary based on vehicle type, duration, and season. In peak season, expect rates between $150 to $250 per day, especially for SUVs or 4WDs.

Insurance and Coverage

Review your personal auto insurance and credit card benefits to determine if they cover rental cars. If not, consider purchasing coverage from the rental agency.

Driving Conditions

Alaska's roads range from well-maintained highways to gravel paths. Ensure your rental agreement permits travel on all intended routes, especially if exploring remote areas.

Age Requirements

Most agencies require drivers to be at least 21 years old, with some charging additional fees for drivers under 25.

Fueling Up

Gas stations can be sparse in remote regions. Always keep your tank full when venturing into less populated areas.

Returning the Vehicle

Return the car with the agreed-upon fuel level to avoid extra charges. Inspect the vehicle with a company representative to confirm its condition upon return.

B. Public Transportation

Alaska's vast landscapes and dispersed communities make public transportation options limited but available in certain areas. Here's an overview to help you navigate the state:

Urban Public Transit

- Anchorage: The People Mover bus system serves Anchorage and parts of Eagle River, operating daily with routes connecting major areas. Fares are affordable, and schedules are available on their [official website](https://www.muni.org/Departments/transit/PeopleMover/Pages/default.aspx).

- **Fairbanks:** The MACS Transit system offers bus services within Fairbanks and North Pole, with routes covering key destinations. Details can be found on the [MACS Transit website](https://www.fnsb.gov/175/Metropolitan-Area-Commuter-System-MACS).

Intercity Bus Services

For travel between cities, several motorcoach services operate during the summer months:

- Alaska Park Connection Motorcoach: Provides daily services between Anchorage, Seward, Talkeetna, and Denali National Park. Reservations are recommended, and schedules are available on their [website](https://www.alaskacoach.com/).

- Interior Alaska Bus Line: Offers year-round services connecting Anchorage, Fairbanks, Tok, and Northway. Reservations are required; more information is on their [website](http://www.interioralaskabusline.com/).

Rail Services

The Alaska Railroad offers scenic routes connecting major destinations:

- Routes: Services include the Denali Star (Anchorage to Fairbanks), Coastal Classic (Anchorage to Seward), and Glacier Discovery (Anchorage to Whittier).

- Schedules and Fares: Operating primarily from mid-May to mid-September, with limited winter services. Details are on the [Alaska Railroad website](https://www.alaskarailroad.com/).

Ferry Services

The Alaska Marine Highway System connects coastal communities:

- Routes: Ferries operate from Bellingham, WA, through Southeast Alaska to Southcentral regions.

- Reservations: Advance booking is essential, especially during peak seasons. Information is available on the [Alaska Marine Highway website](https://dot.alaska.gov/amhs/).

Ride-Sharing and Taxis

In urban areas like Anchorage and Fairbanks, ride-sharing services (e.g., Uber, Lyft) and taxis are available. Availability may be limited in smaller communities.

Considerations

- <u>Seasonality:</u> Many services operate seasonally, primarily in summer. Check current schedules before planning.

- <u>Advance Booking:</u> Due to limited capacity, especially in peak tourist season, advance reservations are advisable.

- <u>Accessibility:</u> Public transportation options are more accessible in urban centers; rural and remote areas may require alternative arrangements.

Chapter 9: Resources

A. Tourist Information Centres

When exploring Alaska, Tourist Information Centers are invaluable for planning and enhancing your journey. These centers offer insights into local attractions, activities, accommodations, and more. Here's a guide to some key centers across the state:

Anchorage

- Visit Anchorage Information Centers: Located downtown and at the Anchorage International Airport, these centers provide expert advice on local attractions, dining, and events. The downtown center is open daily from 9 a.m. to 5 p.m. Contact them at (907) 257-2363 or via email at alocal@anchorage.net.

- Anchorage Alaska Public Lands Information Center (AAPLIC): Situated at 605 W. 4th Avenue, Suite 105, this center offers information on Alaska's public lands, including maps and educational programs. Open Monday through Friday, 9 a.m. to 5 p.m. Reach them at (907) 644-3661.

Fairbanks

- <u>Explore Fairbanks Visitor Center:</u> Located at 101 Dunkel Street, Suite 111, this center provides resources on local attractions, accommodations, and events. Open Monday through Friday, 8 a.m. to 5 p.m. Contact them at (907) 456-5774 or info@explorefairbanks.com.

Juneau

- <u>Juneau Convention & Visitors Bureau:</u> Offers information on local tours, dining, and accommodations. Visit their website at [www.traveljuneau.com] or call (907) 586-2201.

Ketchikan

- <u>Southeast Alaska Discovery Center:</u> Located at 50 Main Street, this center provides exhibits on the region's natural and cultural history. Open Tuesday through Saturday, 8 a.m. to 4 p.m. Contact them at (907) 228-6220.

Skagway

- <u>Skagway Visitor Information Center:</u> Situated at 245 Broadway, this center offers insights into local history, tours, and attractions. Open daily during the summer months. Contact them at (907) 983-2854.

Statewide Resources

- <u>Alaska Public Lands Information Centers:</u>
  With locations in Anchorage, Fairbanks,
  Ketchikan, and Tok, these centers provide
  comprehensive information on Alaska's
  public   lands.   Visit
  [www.alaskacenters.gov] for more details.

Tips for Visiting

- <u>Operating Hours:</u> Hours may vary
  seasonally; it's advisable to check ahead.

- <u>Services Offered:</u> Centers typically
  provide   maps,   brochures,   and
  personalized recommendations.

- <u>Local Insights:</u> Staff can offer current
  information   on   events,   weather
  conditions, and travel advisories.

B. Emergency Contacts and Health Services

When exploring Alaska, it's essential to have
access to reliable emergency contacts and health
services to ensure a safe and enjoyable journey.
Here's a comprehensive guide to key resources
available throughout the state:

Emergency Contacts

- <u>General Emergencies:</u> For immediate assistance from law enforcement, fire services, or medical emergencies, dial 911.

- <u>Alaska State Troopers:</u> For non-emergency situations requiring state law enforcement, contact the Alaska State Troopers at (907) 269-5511.

- <u>Alaska Careline:</u> If you or someone you know is experiencing a mental health crisis, call the Alaska Careline at 1-877-266-4357 (HELP) or visit [www.carelinealaska.com].

Health Services

- <u>Hospitals and Clinics:</u> Alaska has numerous hospitals and clinics across its regions. Major facilities include:

- <u>Providence Alaska Medical Center (Anchorage):</u> The largest hospital in the state, offering comprehensive medical services. Contact: (907) 562-2211.

- <u>Fairbanks Memorial Hospital (Fairbanks):</u> Provides a wide range of healthcare services. Contact: (907) 452-8181.

- <u>Bartlett Regional Hospital (Juneau):</u> Offers medical services to the Southeast Alaska region. Contact: (907) 796-8900.

- Public Health Centers: The Alaska Department of Health operates public health centers providing immunizations, health education, and other services. Find a center near you at [health.alaska.gov/dph/Nursing/Pages/locations.aspx].

Travel Health Tips

- Travel Insurance: It's advisable to have travel insurance that covers medical emergencies, especially if you plan to engage in adventure activities.

- Medications: Ensure you bring an adequate supply of any prescription medications, as some areas may have limited pharmacy services.

- Vaccinations: Check with your healthcare provider about recommended vaccinations before traveling to Alaska.

Additional Resources

- Alaska 2-1-1: For information on health and human services, dial 2-1-1 or visit [www.alaska211.org].

- Alaska Department of Health and Social Services: Provides comprehensive information on health services and emergency preparedness. Visit [health.alaska.gov].

C. Useful Apps and Websites for Travelers

When planning your Alaskan adventure, equipping yourself with the right digital tools can significantly enhance your experience. Here are some essential apps and websites to consider:

1. The Alaska App

This comprehensive guide offers information on lodging, dining, attractions, and more. It functions offline, making it invaluable in areas with limited connectivity. Available for both iOS and Android devices.

2. The MILEPOST®

Known as the "Bible of North Country Travel," this app provides detailed information on highways, services, and attractions across Alaska. It's particularly useful for road trips.

3. AllTrails

For hiking enthusiasts, AllTrails offers a vast collection of trail maps, reviews, and photos. It helps you discover trails suited to your skill level and interests. Available on iOS and Android.

4. My Aurora Forecast & Alerts

If witnessing the Northern Lights is on your agenda, this app provides real-time aurora forecasts and alerts, increasing your chances of a successful sighting. Available on iOS and Android.

5. Alaska.org

This website offers expert advice, trip ideas, and detailed information on destinations and activities throughout Alaska. It's a valuable resource for planning your itinerary.

6. Travel Alaska Guide App

This app provides city guides for major Alaskan cities, including Anchorage, Fairbanks, and Juneau. It functions offline, which is beneficial in remote areas. Available on iOS and Android.

7. PeakFinder

For mountain enthusiasts, PeakFinder identifies surrounding peaks using your device's camera, enhancing your appreciation of Alaska's rugged landscapes. Available on iOS and Android.

8. Night Sky

This app allows you to identify stars, planets, and constellations, enriching your stargazing experiences in Alaska's clear night skies. Available on iOS and Android.

Conclusion

Congratulations on choosing the **Alaska Travel Guide 2025**! We're delighted you selected this book to help you navigate one of the world's most breathtaking destinations. Alaska is a place of incredible beauty, rugged landscapes, and unique experiences, and we hope this guide has made your journey smoother, richer, and more memorable.

In these pages, we've explored Alaska's iconic destinations—from the bustling city of Anchorage to the serene wilderness of Denali National Park, and from the coastal treasures of the Kenai Peninsula to the charming towns like Fairbanks and Juneau. Each location has its own charm, and we hope our insights have helped you experience these places in ways that are meaningful to you.

This guide introduced you to Alaska's diverse wildlife, guiding you to the best spots for sightings of grizzly bears, whales, eagles, and more. Alaska's nature is majestic and untamed, offering outdoor adventures like hiking, fishing, and winter sports that bring you closer to the land. We hope you've enjoyed discovering this wild beauty in ways that excite and inspire.

But Alaska isn't only about landscapes and wildlife. It's also a land of rich history and culture. From the traditions of Alaska's Indigenous people to the stories of gold rush pioneers, Alaska has a past that adds depth to its natural wonders. We hope learning about its heritage has made your visit even more fulfilling.

We've also provided practical tips to make your travels easier, from choosing accommodations to navigating transportation. Whether you chose to stay in cozy lodges, camp under the stars, or explore by RV, we hope our suggestions helped you enjoy Alaska comfortably and authentically.

As you leave, we hope you carry memories of Alaska's towering mountains, vast wilderness, and the peaceful moments that make this state unforgettable. Alaska is more than a place to visit—it's an experience that stays with you, filling you with a sense of awe, tranquility, and adventure.

Thank you for letting the Alaska Travel Guide 2025 be part of your journey. May the spirit of Alaska remain with you, and may your adventures continue to bring you closer to the wonders of our world. Safe travels, and we hope to see you back in Alaska soon!

Warm regards,

The Alaska Travel Guide Team

Bonus: Authentic Alaskan Recipes

As a special treat, we're delighted to share some of Alaska's most cherished traditional recipes. Each dish reflects the rugged beauty and rich natural resources of Alaska, from fresh salmon and wild game to wild berries that flourish in the summer months. These recipes capture the essence of Alaskan cuisine—hearty, comforting, and deeply connected to the land and sea.

1. Alaskan Salmon Chowder

A comforting, creamy chowder that features Alaska's famous wild salmon. This dish is perfect for chilly days and showcases the delicate flavour of fresh, local fish.

Ingredients:
- 500g wild-caught salmon, cut into chunks
- 1 medium onion, diced
- 3 medium potatoes, peeled and cubed
- 2 carrots, diced
- 1 stalk celery, chopped
- 1 liter fish or vegetable stock
- 250ml heavy cream
- 2 tbsp butter
- 1 bay leaf
- Salt and pepper to taste
- Fresh dill for garnish

Instructions:
1. In a large pot, melt butter over medium heat. Add onion, carrot, and celery, and sauté until softened.
2. Add the potatoes, fish stock, and bay leaf. Bring to a simmer and cook for 10-15 minutes, or until potatoes are tender.
3. Gently add the salmon pieces and simmer for an additional 5-7 minutes until cooked through.
4. Stir in the cream and season with salt and pepper. Remove the bay leaf before serving.
5. Garnish with fresh dill and serve hot with crusty bread or crackers.

2. Reindeer Stew (Sauted Reindeer)
A hearty, flavourful stew that highlights Alaska's wild game. Substitute with venison or beef if reindeer isn't available.

Ingredients:
- 500g reindeer or venison, cubed
- 3 large potatoes, cubed
- 2 carrots, sliced
- 1 onion, diced
- 2 cups mushrooms, sliced
- 1 liter beef or game stock
- 1 tbsp flour
- 1 tbsp vegetable oil
- Salt and pepper to taste
- Fresh thyme for garnish

Instructions:

1. Heat oil in a large pot over medium-high heat. Brown the meat, then set aside.
2. In the same pot, add the onion and mushrooms, sautéing until soft.
3. Sprinkle flour over the vegetables and stir well.
4. Return the meat to the pot, add the stock, potatoes, and carrots, and bring to a boil.
5. Lower the heat, cover, and let simmer for 1.5-2 hours, or until the meat is tender.
6. Season with salt and pepper. Garnish with thyme and serve with crusty bread or over mashed potatoes.

3. Alaskan Sourdough Pancakes

These classic sourdough pancakes have been a breakfast staple in Alaska since the gold rush era. They're fluffy, tangy, and best enjoyed with Alaska's wild berry syrup.

Ingredients:
- 1 cup sourdough starter
- 1 cup flour
- 1 cup milk
- 1 egg
- 1 tbsp sugar
- 1 tsp baking soda
- 1/4 tsp salt
- Butter for cooking
- Wild berry syrup or maple syrup for serving

Instructions:

1. In a large bowl, mix the sourdough starter, flour, and milk until combined. Let sit for at least 30 minutes or overnight for a more tangy flavour.
2. Add the egg, sugar, baking soda, and salt to the mixture, stirring until smooth.
3. Heat a griddle or skillet over medium heat and lightly grease with butter.
4. Pour batter onto the griddle, cooking until bubbles form on the surface, then flip and cook until golden brown.
5. Serve hot with wild berry syrup or maple syrup.

4. Alaskan King Crab Legs with Garlic Butter

A true Alaskan delicacy, these succulent crab legs are perfect for a special occasion. Serve with garlic butter for a luxurious treat.

Ingredients:
- 1kg Alaskan King Crab legs
- 1/2 cup unsalted butter
- 3 garlic cloves, minced
- Fresh lemon wedges
- Fresh parsley, chopped, for garnish

Instructions:
1. Fill a large pot with water, bring to a boil, and carefully add the crab legs. Boil for 4-5 minutes until heated through.
2. In a small saucepan, melt the butter over low heat. Add the minced garlic and cook until fragrant.

3. Remove the crab legs and drain. Serve with garlic butter, lemon wedges, and garnish with parsley.

5. Wild Berry Cobbler

Alaska's summer is full of wild berries, like blueberries, lingonberries, and salmonberries. This cobbler is a delicious way to enjoy them, especially with a scoop of ice cream.

Ingredients:
- 4 cups mixed wild berries
- 1/2 cup sugar
- 1 tbsp lemon juice
- 1 tbsp cornstarch
- 1 cup flour
- 1/2 cup sugar
- 1/2 cup milk
- 1/4 cup butter, melted
- 1 tsp baking powder
- Pinch of salt

Instructions:
1. Preheat oven to 180°C (350°F). In a bowl, combine berries, 1/2 cup sugar, lemon juice, and cornstarch, then spread evenly in a baking dish.
2. In a separate bowl, mix the flour, remaining sugar, baking powder, and salt. Stir in the milk and melted butter to form a batter.
3. Pour the batter over the berry mixture, spreading gently.
4. Bake for 35-40 minutes, until the top is golden. Serve warm with a scoop of ice cream.

Made in the USA
Columbia, SC
22 March 2025